I0469775

Waterloo Ontario Book 2 in Colour Photos, Saving Our History One Photo at a Time

Photography
by Barbara Raué
updated 2016

Series Name:
Cruising Ontario

Book 115: Waterloo Book 2
Mary Allen Neighbourhood

Cover photo: 73 George Street, Page 32

Series Name: Cruising Ontario
Saving Our History One Photo at a Time
in colour photos

Book 33: Southampton

Book 34: Jarvis

Book 35: Hagersville

Book 36: Caledonia

Book 37: Simcoe

Book 38-41: Cambridge

Book 42-43: Kitchener

Book 44: Drumbo

Book 45: Sheffield

Book 46: Shelburne

Book 47: Alton, Mono

Book 48: London Colour

Book 49: St. Thomas

Book 50-52: Orangeville

Book 53-55: Dundas

Book 56: Stratford

Book 57: Hanover

Book 58-59: New Hamburg

Book 60: Waterdown

Book 61: Burlington

Book 62: Stoney Creek

Book 63: Seaforth

Book 64: Aberfoyle, Morriston and Rockton

Book 65: Eden Mills

Book 66: Ancaster and Mount Hope

Book 67: Jarvis,Pt.Dover

Book 68-69: Fergus, Elora

Book 70-71: Elmira

Book72:St.Jacobs, St.Clements, Heidelberg,Crosshill,Bamberg

Book 73: Linwood, Macton

Book 74: Wellesley

Book 75: Listowel

Book 76: Palmerston

Book 77:Dorchester to Aylmer

Book 78-79: Aylmer

Book 80: Drayton & Area

Book 81: Tillsonburg

Book 82: Arthur

Book 83: Rockwood

Book 84: Acton

Book 85-86: Guelph

Book 87-91: Hamilton

Book 92-93: Owen Sound

Book 94: Oakville

Book 95: Brantford

Book 96: Mount Forest

Book 97: Orillia

Book 98: Ayr

Book 99-101: Peterborough

Book 102-104: Niagara on Lake

Book105:Harriston,Clifford

Book 106: Neustadt

Book 107-108: Port Elgin

Book 109: Wingham, Blyth

Book 110:Lucknow,Mitchell

Book 111: Conestogo, Bloomingdale

Book 112: Delhi

Book 113: Waterford

Book 114-116: Waterloo

Other Books by Barbara Raue

Coins of Gold

Arrows, Indians and Love

The Life and Times of Barbara
Volume 1: Inventions That Have Enhanced My Life
Volume 2: Entertainment That I Have Enjoyed
Volume 3: East Coast Trips
Volume 4: Olympics Have Always Intrigued Me
Volume 5: Wonders of the World
Volume 6: Caribbean Cruises We Have Enjoyed
Volume 7: Animals
Volume 8: Storms and Other Major Disasters in My Lifetime
Volume 9: Wars, Terrorist Attacks and Major Disasters

The Cromwell Family Book

Laura Secord Discovered

Daddy Where Are You? – a memoir

Visit Barbara's website to view all of her books
http://barbararaue.ca

Waterloo is a city in Southern Ontario. The Conestogo Parkway and Highway 8 connect Waterloo with Kitchener, Cambridge, Highway 7/8, and Highway 401. Waterloo shares several of its north-south arterial roads with neighboring Kitchener. These municipalities surround Waterloo: Wellesley, St. Jacobs, Elmira, Conestogo and West Montrose, Guelph, Cambridge, Kitchener, Stratford, Wilmot and St. Agatha.

Waterloo was built on land that was part of a parcel of 675,000 acres assigned in 1784 to the Iroquois alliance that made up the League of Six Nations. Almost immediately, the native groups began to sell some of the land. Between 1796 and 1798, 93,000 acres were sold through a Crown Grant to Richard Beasley, with the Six Nations Indians continuing to hold the mortgage on the lands.

The first immigrants to the area were Mennonites from Pennsylvania. They bought deeds to land parcels from Beasley and began moving into the area in 1804. The following year, a group of twenty-six Mennonites pooled resources to purchase all of the unsold land from Beasley and discharge the mortgage held by the Six Nations Indians.

The Mennonites divided the land into smaller lots; two lots initially owned by Abraham Erb became the central core of Waterloo. Erb built a sawmill on Beaver, now Laurel, Creek in 1808 and in 1816 built the area's first grist mill which farmers from miles around used to grind their wheat into flour, a very important staple.

In 1816, the new township was named after Waterloo, Belgium, the site of the Battle of Waterloo, which had ended the Napoleonic Wars in Europe. After that war, the area became a popular destination for German immigrants. By the 1840s, German settlers were the dominant segment of the population. Many Germans settled in the small hamlet to the southeast of Waterloo. In their honor, the village was named Berlin in 1833 (renamed to Kitchener in 1916). Berlin was chosen as the site of the seat for the County of Waterloo in 1853.

The inhabitants established Waterloo as an important industrial and commercial center. The village had a council chamber, fire hall, post office, library, and four steam-powered factories, including the Granite Mills and Distillery which became the Seagram Company.

The Grand River flows southward along the east side of the city. Its most significant tributary within the city is Laurel Creek, whose source lies just to the west of the city limits and its mouth just to the east, and crosses much of the city's central areas including the University of Waterloo lands and Waterloo Park; it flows under the uptown area in a culvert. In the west end of the city, the Waterloo Moraine provides over 300,000 people in the region with drinking water. Much of the gently hilly Waterloo Moraine underlies existing developed areas.

The main campuses of the University of Waterloo and Wilfrid Laurier University are located in Waterloo.

The button manufacturing company of Richard Roschman & Brothers was one of several button manufacturers that once operated in the Kitchener Waterloo region. It was an ideal location for both the importing of raw materials and the exporting of finished product, with the Grand Trunk Railway only meters away. By 1900, the business employed more than one hundred people and its buttons were exported as far away as Europe and Japan. By 1944, the factory's buttons had become obsolete and the factory closed its doors. Between 1944 and 1989, the building housed three other companies. In 1982, the City of Waterloo designated the building as an architecturally significant and historical landmark. The Waterloo Community Arts Centre took over the building in 1993.

In the mid-1800s, intensive wheat farms dominated the agricultural scene in Canada. Wheat and other grains were cut with hand-held scythes, tied in sheaves, and stacked in stooks. When dry, the stooks were hauled in wagons to the farmyard and threshed or flailed to separate the grain from the stalk. Then the grain was winnowed to separate the kernels from the chaff.

In 1834 a Virginia farmer, Cyrus McCormick, patented a machine to cut and collect grain. The McCormick Reaper gathered and cut the stalks and pushed them onto a tray. The grain still had to be tied, stacked, threshed, and winnowed by hand, but McCormick's success at farm mechanization encouraged other inventors. By the 1850s, small portable threshing machines powered by animal-driven treadmills were available.

In Waterloo, enterprising blacksmiths saw the sales potential for reliable farm equipment. In the 1850s and 1860s the foundries of Abraham Buehler on Erb Street West and Jacob Bricker at King Street near Weaver produced plows, threshing machines, separators, and other implements. Buehler's foundry was eventually purchased by Absalom Merner of New Hamburg, whose brother owned the Elmira Agricultural Implements Company. In 1888 Merner joined with Elias W.B. Snider to create the Waterloo Manufacturing Company. Snider also owned a mill in St. Jacobs that processed local and western wheat into high quality flour for sale in Ontario and Eastern Canada. By 1906, Snider was sole owner of the Waterloo Manufacturing Company.

Western Canada was a new market for agricultural equipment as farmers were beginning to tame the wild prairie grasslands and plant wheat and other grain crops. The Waterloo Manufacturing Company offered machinery to replace slow, inefficient hand labor. The threshing machine threshed and pummeled the wheat and removed the grain from the stalk.

The Waterloo steam traction engine replaced the wooden horse-powers. The heavy locomotive-style boiler machines were hauled by horses, mules or oxen from farm to farm and fueled by wood, coal, straw or kerosene.

As the years passed the company added new products and sent the "Waterloo" name across the continent. Gasoline-powered tractors and combines made traction engines and threshing machines obsolete. With the outbreak of war in 1939, tanks, ships and airplane parts were manufactured here.

After the war the company custom manufactured and built equipment for other companies. With the upsurge in the pulp and paper industry, the company manufactured paper machine rolls. Today the Waterloo Manufacturing Company services boilers.

Table of Contents

Mary Allen Neighborhood

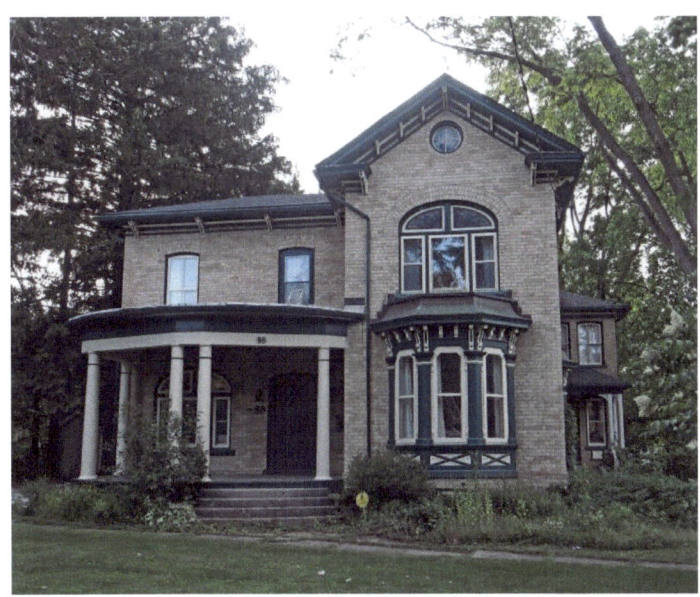

88 William Street West – 1880 – Victorian - 2½ storey projecting rectangular bay, cornice return on gable, bay window with cornice brackets, wraparound verandah, stained glass windows

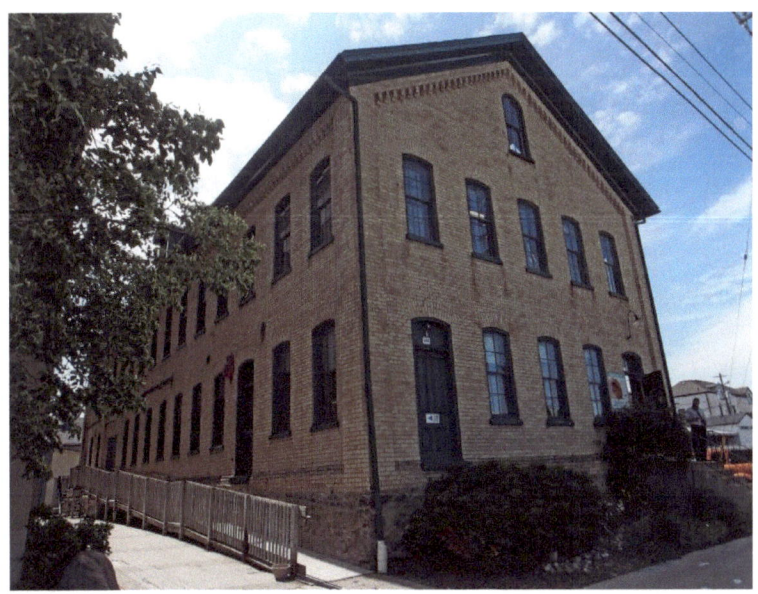

William Street East – bevelled dentil moulding

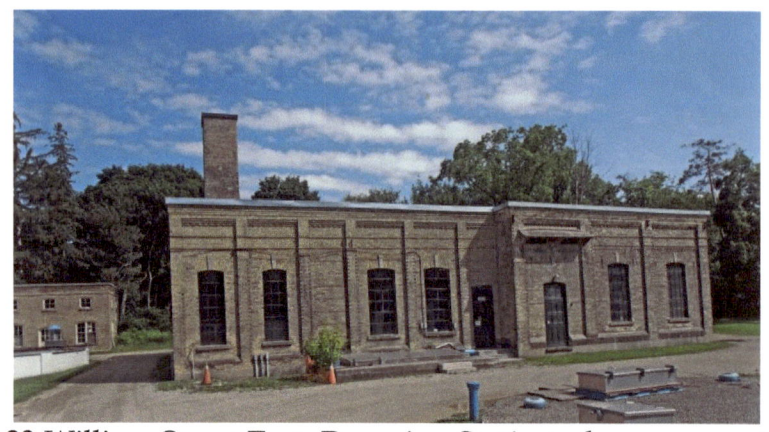

17-23 William Street East, Pumping Station – began operation in 1899 when three artesian wells, yielding a daily flow of 750,000 gallons, were sunk to provide the city with water and fire protection. The Pumping Station in a single storey building in yellow brick in plain Victorian Industrial style. Large, steel-framed windows admit good light to the machinery and operators inside. Each window bay has a shallow buttress rising to a broad corbelled moulding of bricks along the roof line. A stone keystone in the low arch over each window suggests solidity.

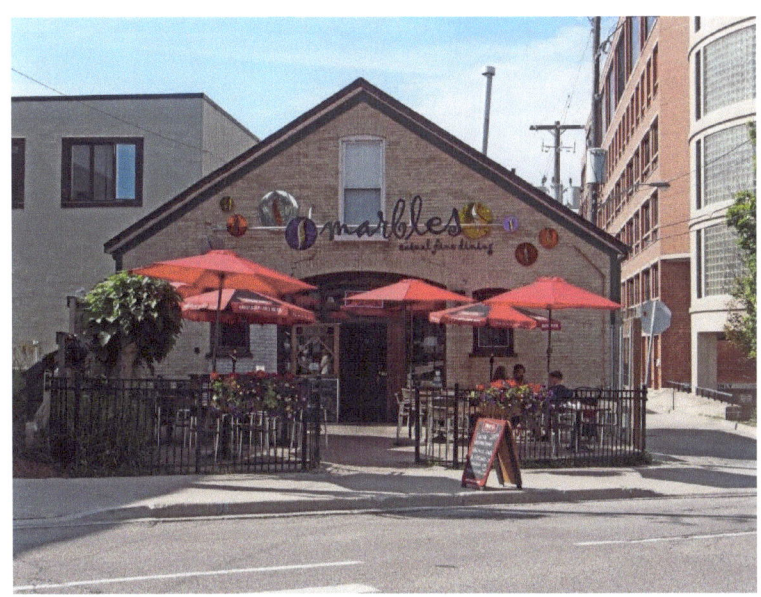

8 William Street East – Vernacular – 1884 – 1½ storey gable to street yellow brick – livery stable for former Alexander Hotel that stood at corner of William Street East & King Street South

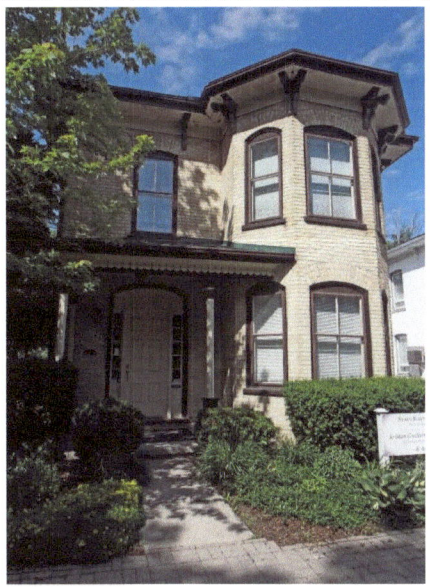

156 King Street South – c. 1880 – Italianate style in yellow brick, 2-storey projecting bay, sidelights and a blind transom around the main entrance; cornice brackets

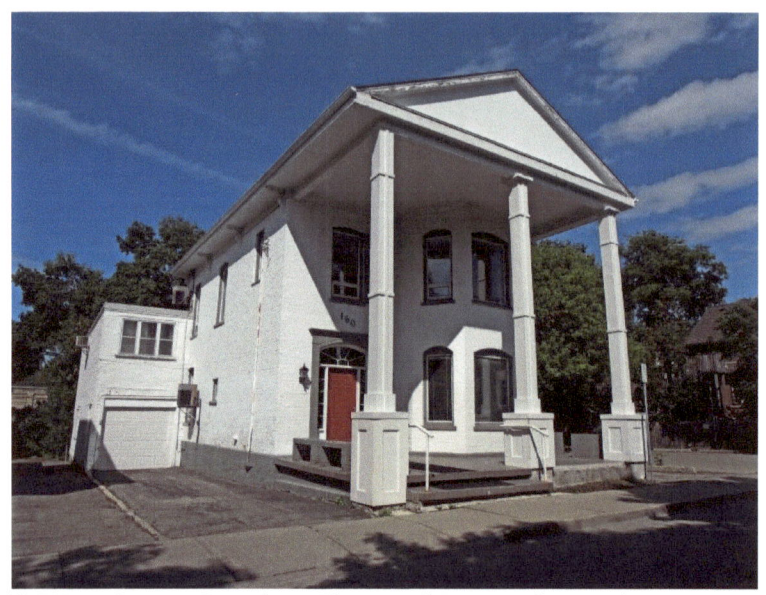

160 King Street South – Classical Revival – pediment, two-storey bay window

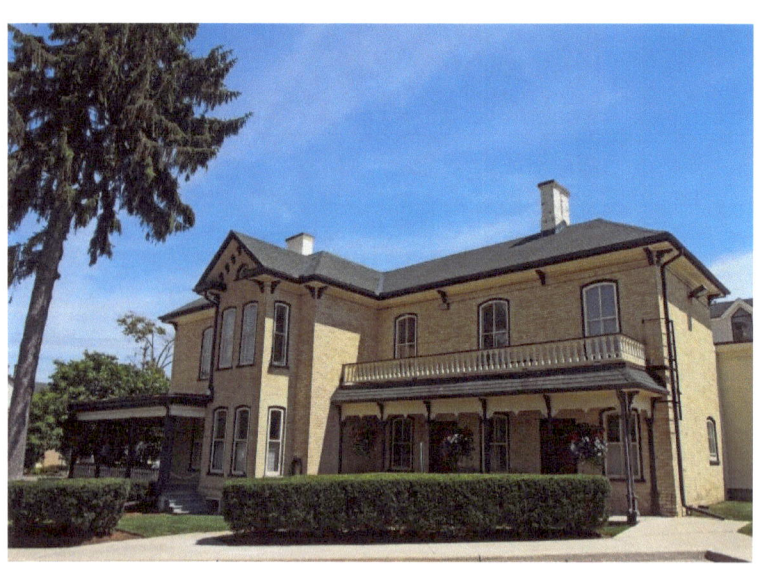

167 King Street South – 1880 - Italianate with 2½ storey tower-like bay, cornice return on gable, brackets, 2nd floor balcony

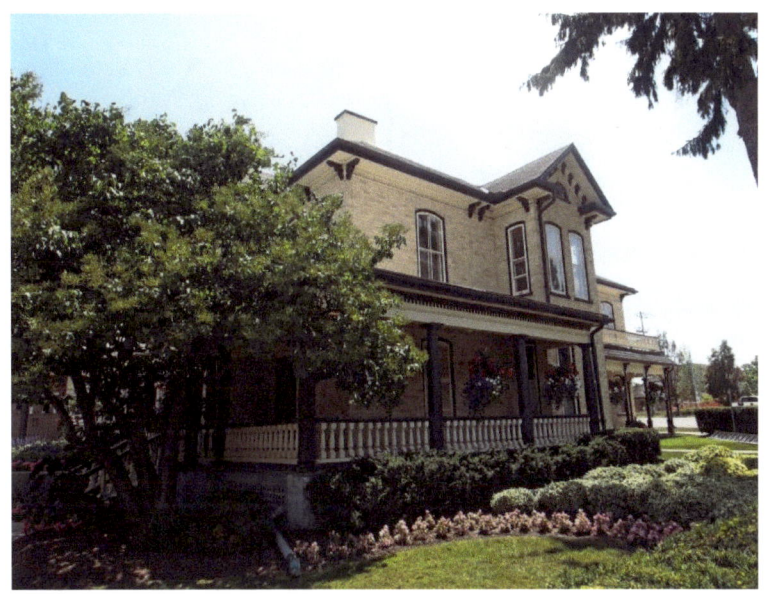

167 King Street South

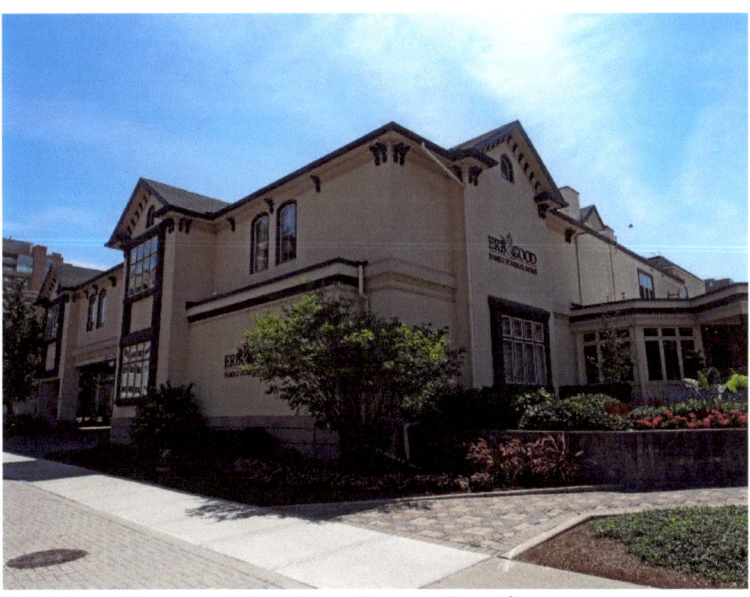

171 King Street South

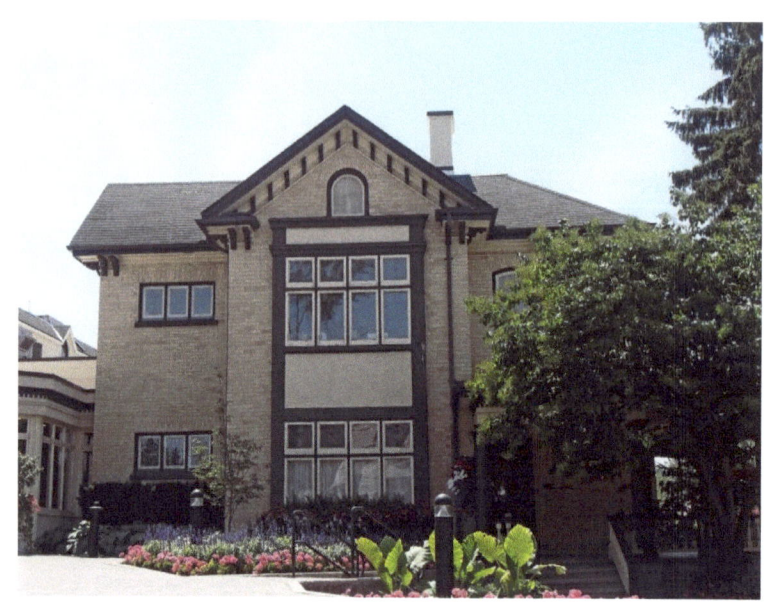

171 King Street South – Erb Good Family Funeral Home

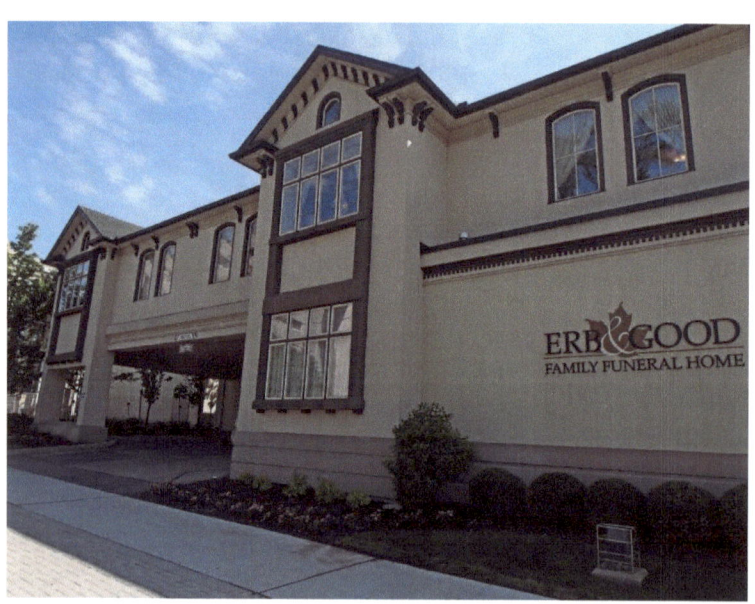

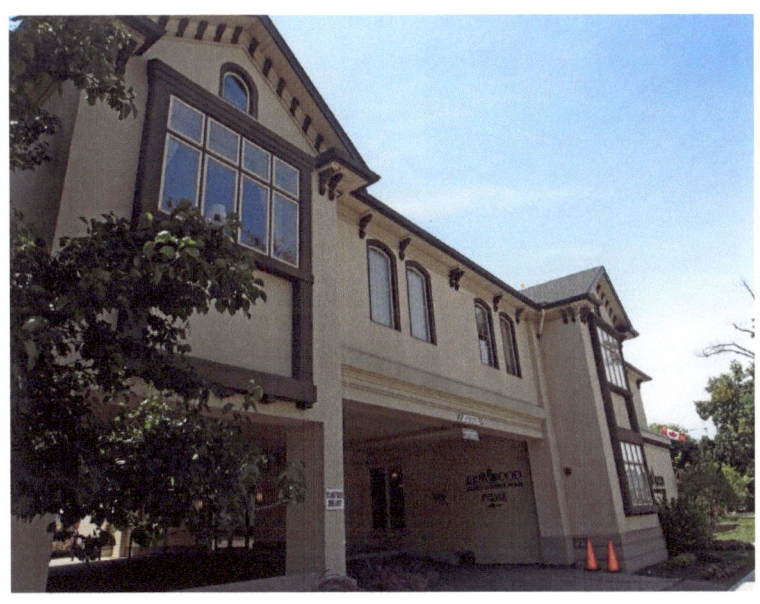

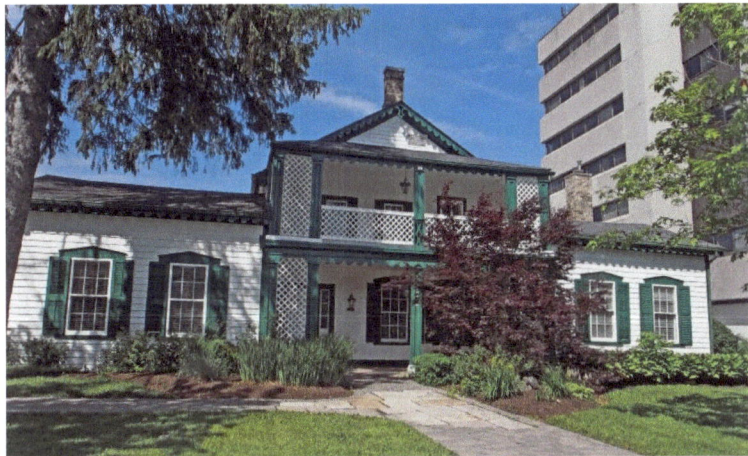

172 King Street South – the original portion, the first homestead in Waterloo, was built about 1812 by Abraham Erb; subsequent additions – white clapboard; wings on either side of centre section and second-storey balcony added 1855; 6-over-6 arrangement of window panes is a Georgian characteristic; symmetrical front porch between two wings with latticework, Gothic bargeboard and Doric columns reflects a Regency influence.

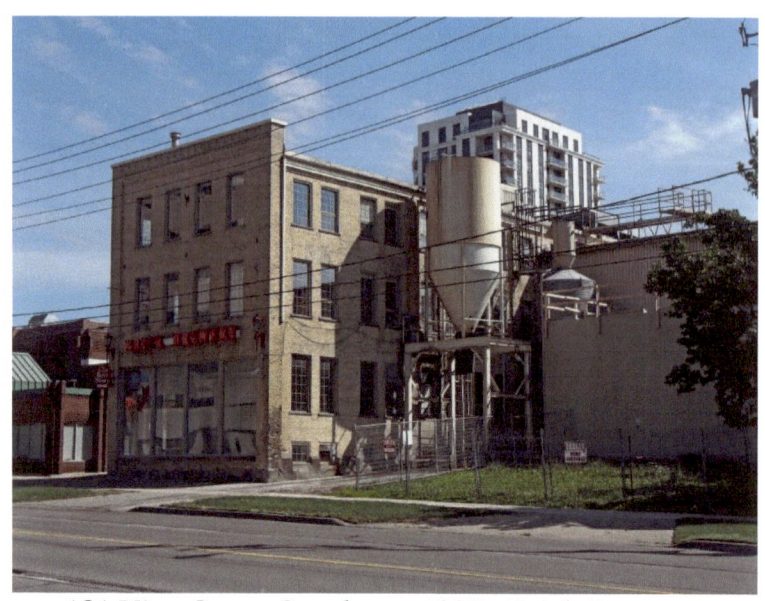

181 King Street South – c. 1905 - Brick Brewery

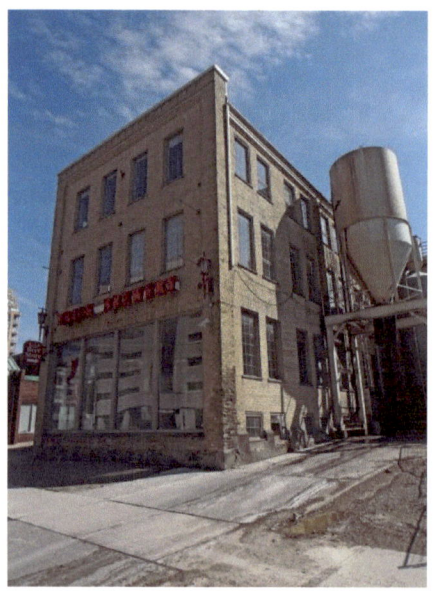

Brick Brewery – former furniture factory converted into a
traditional European Brew house

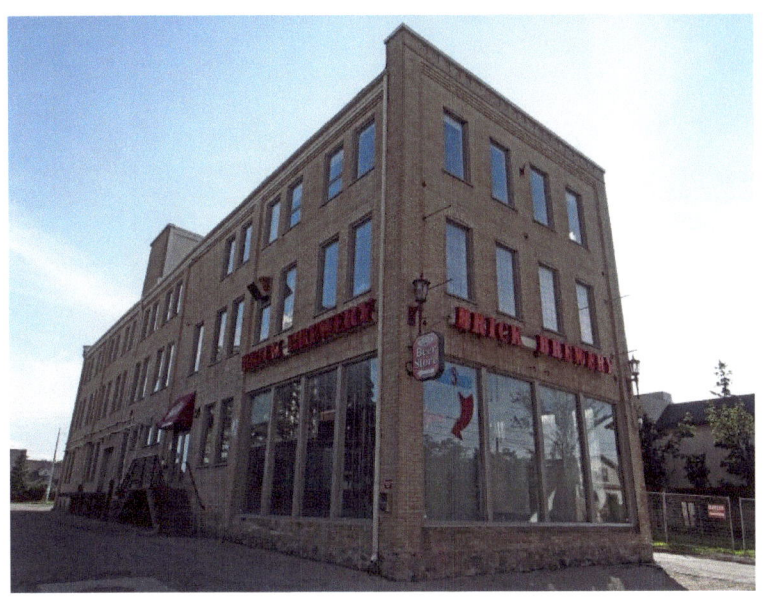

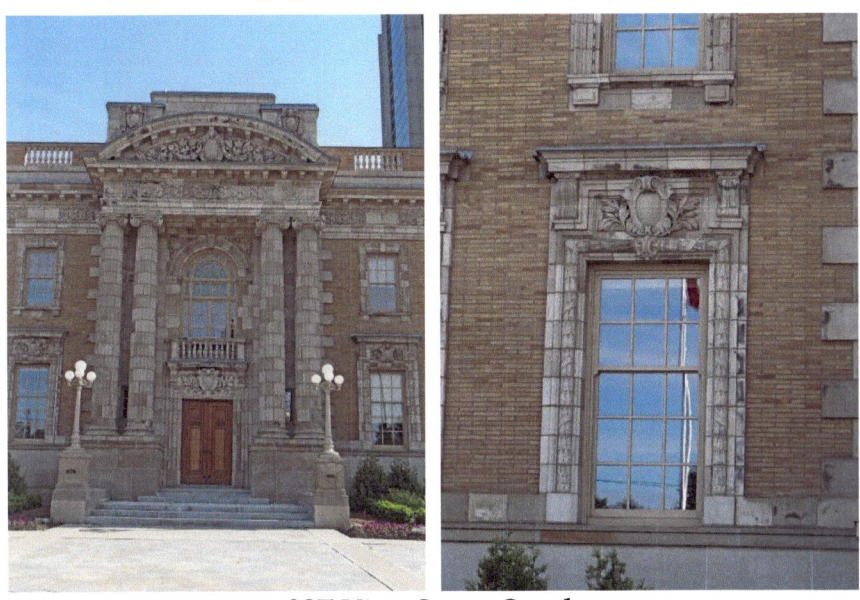

227 King Street South

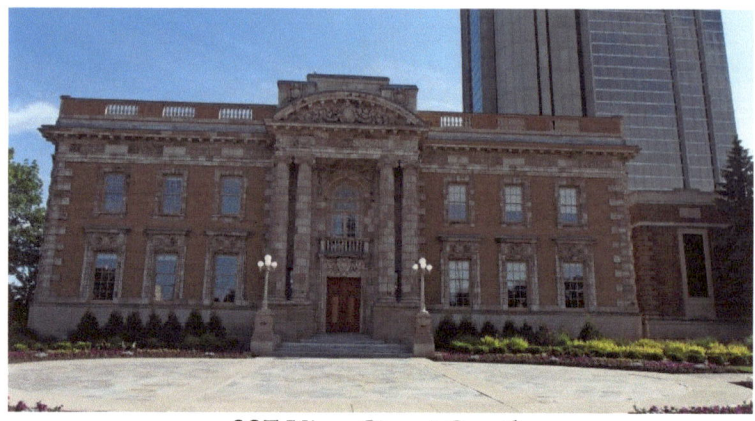

227 King Street South

The head office of The Mutual Life Assurance Company of Canada (now head office of Sun Life Financial's Canadian operations) was completed in 1912. The Renaissance Revival style building is ornamented with features such as the two-storey fluted paired Ionic columns supporting a large segmental arch above the main doors, elaborate window surrounds, and a parapet with a balustrade. It is clad in light brown and yellow Roman brick, and embellished with projecting pedimented bays and quoins. Many of the decorative details on the façade are made from imported English terra cotta. Situated within a Beaux Arts designed landscape, the building is a unique and iconic corporate pavilion. The monumental scale of the building and its rich ornamentation symbolize the importance and stability of Waterloo's first life insurance company and reflect the town's early twentieth century prosperity and sense of civic pride.

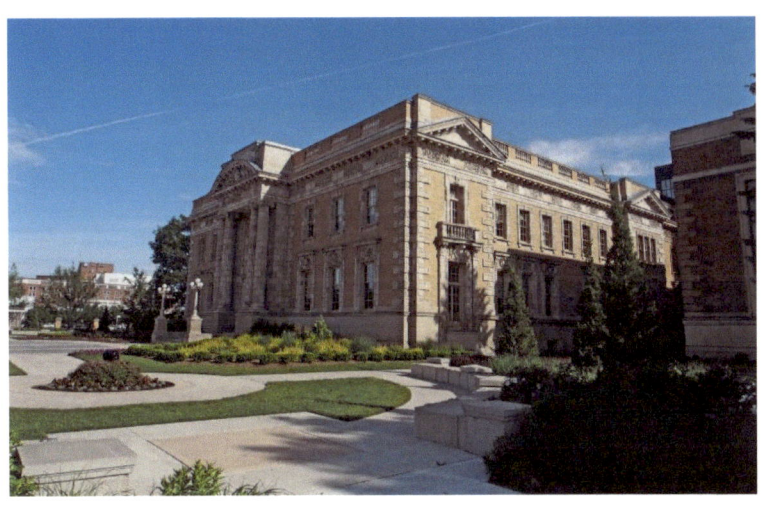

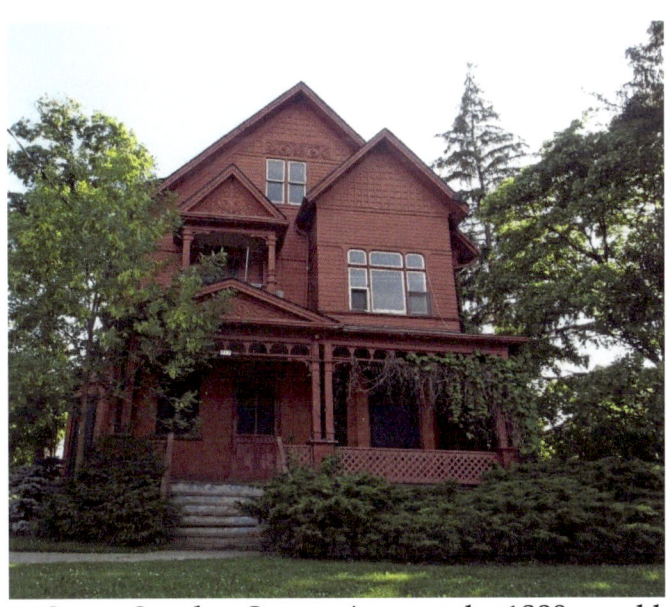

217 King Street South – Queen Anne style, 1889 – red brick 1st storey, 2nd storey siding, shingle siding in attic gables

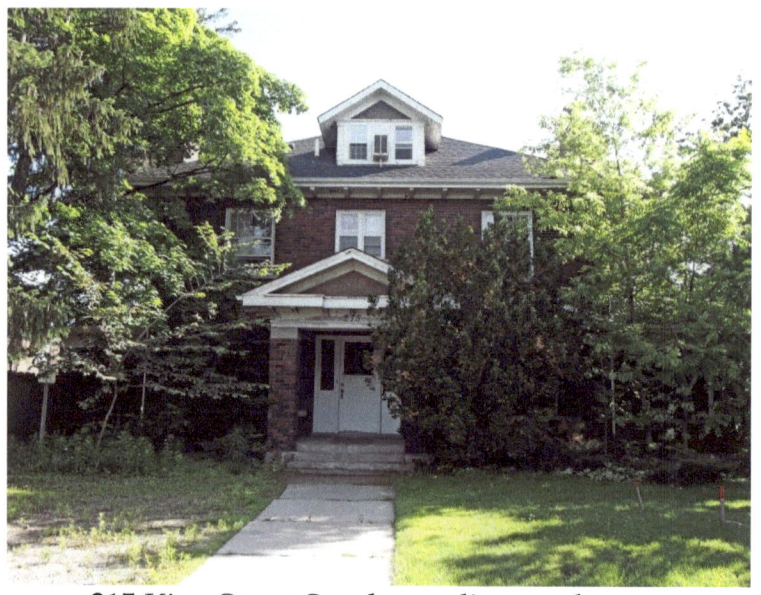

215 King Street South – pediment, dormer

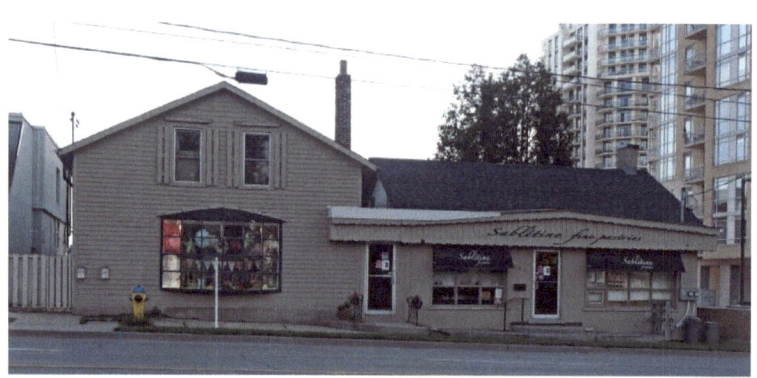

205 King Street South – Vernacular – 1849 – 1½ storey frame
203 King Street South – Vernacular – 1855 – early frame
dwelling – both are now commercial

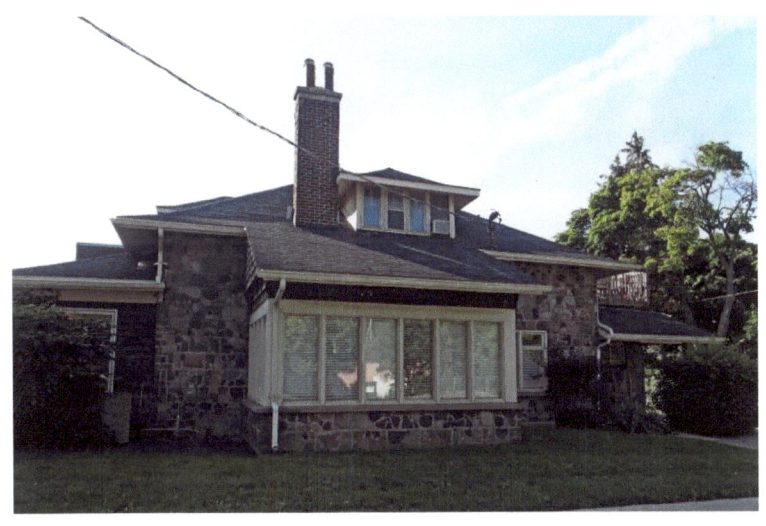

208 King Street South – Arts and Crafts style with brick and stone - 1924

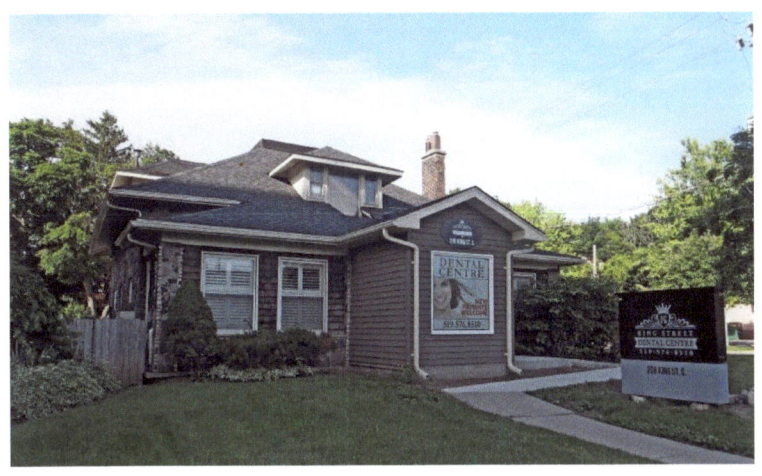

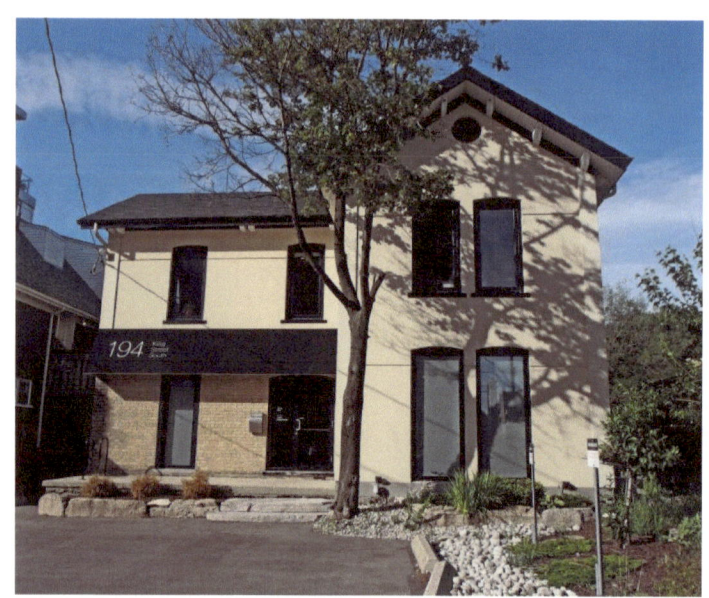

194 King Street South

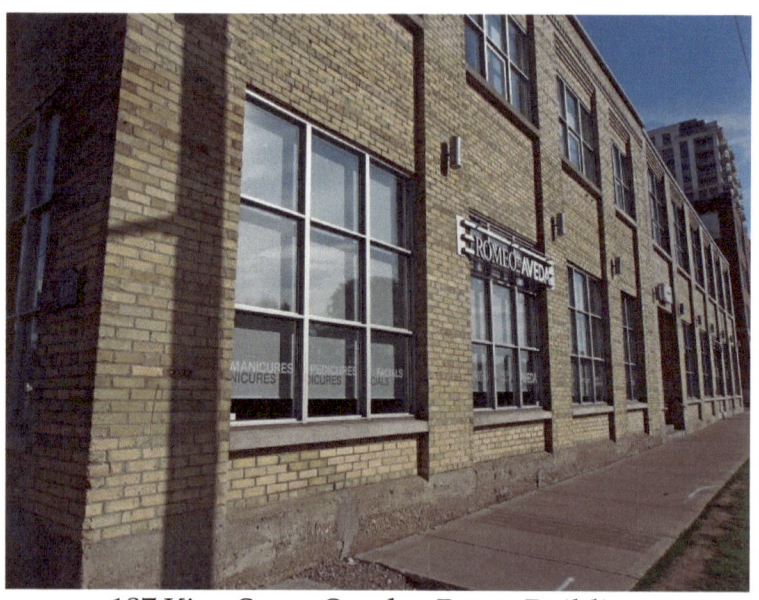

187 King Street South – Bauer Building

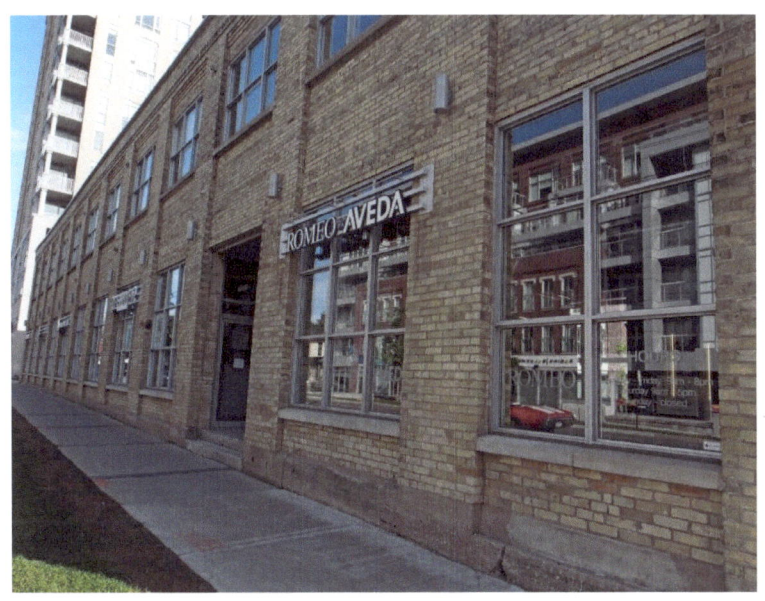

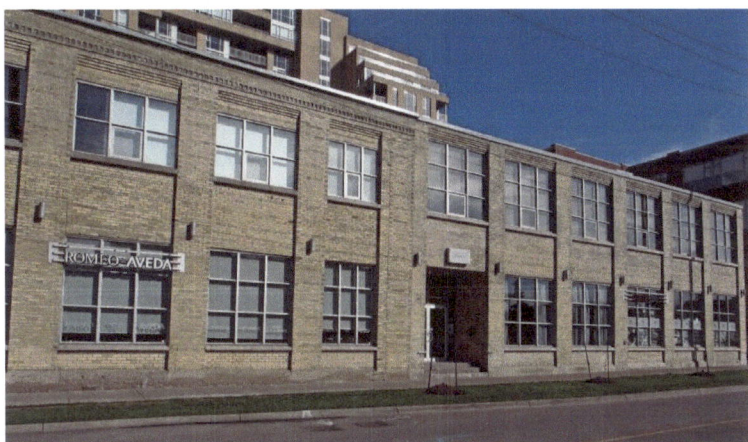

187 King Street South – Bauer Building
Aloyes Bauer started out in 1888 operating a carriage business then moved on to a simple cotton upholstering plant; later it was a major automotive products supplier; now it is being converted into residential/commercial use

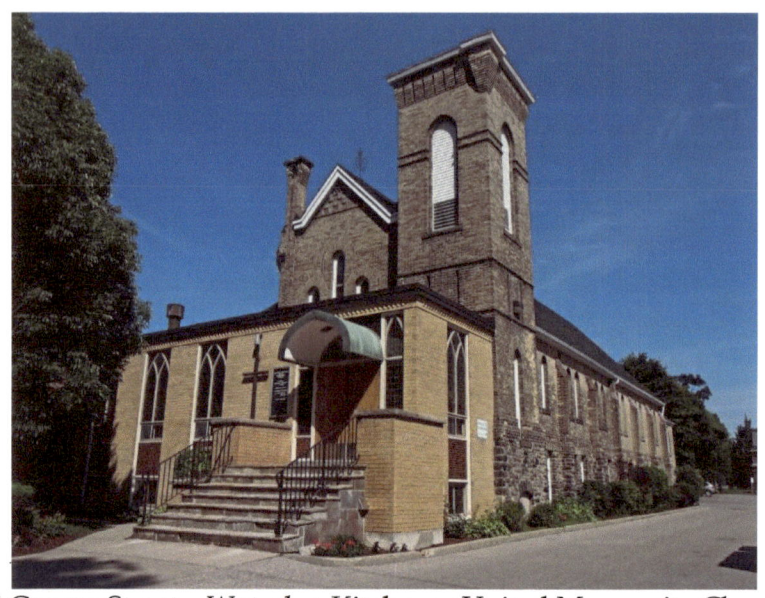

15 George Street – Waterloo Kitchener United Mennonite Church

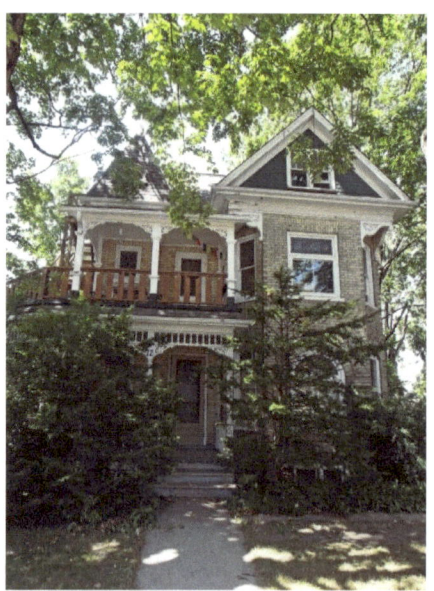

12 George Street – Victorian style built in 1907 – two-storey verandah with delicate wood-turned elements, turret, stained glass windows

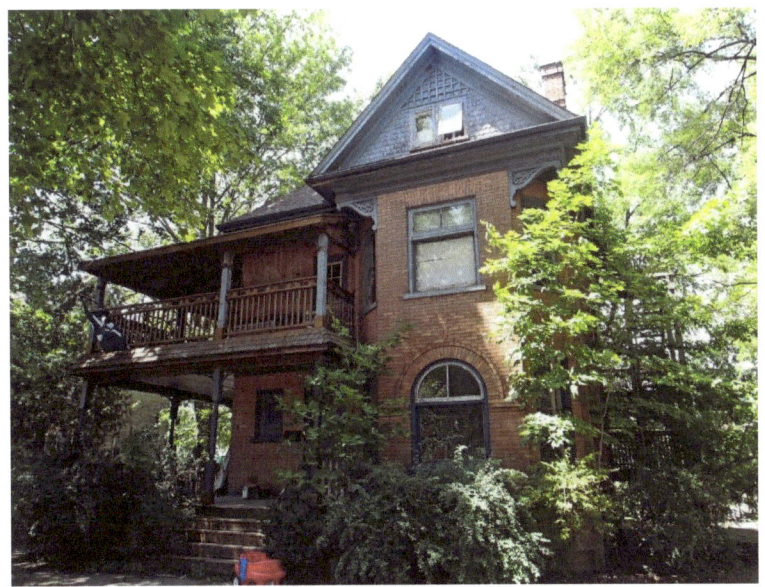

16 George Street – Victorian style, two-storey verandah, Romanesque style window arch

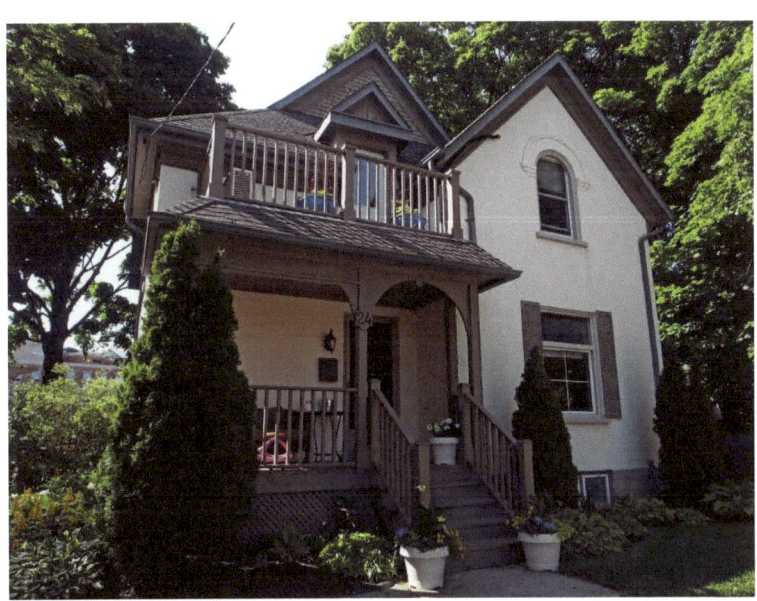

24 George Street – Queen Anne style, 2nd floor balcony

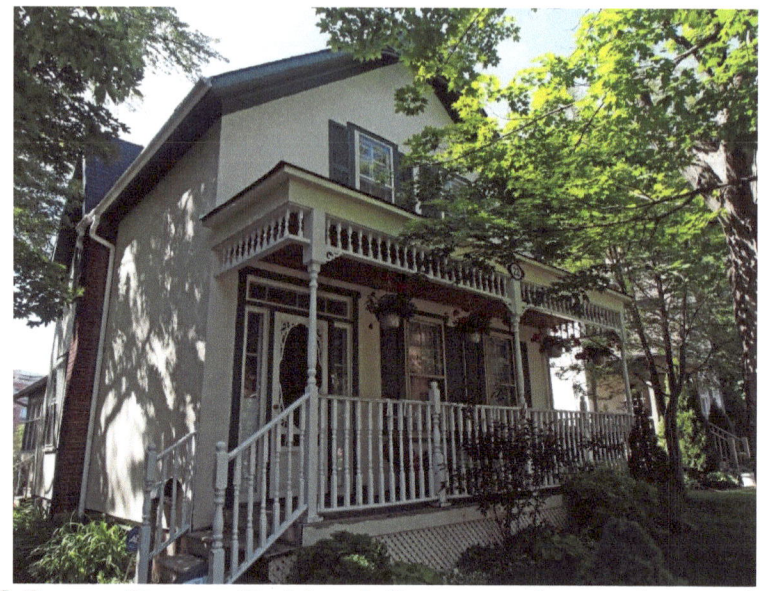

22 George Street – Gothic - delicate wood-turned verandah

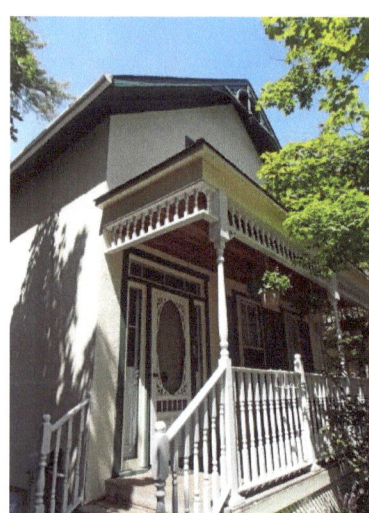

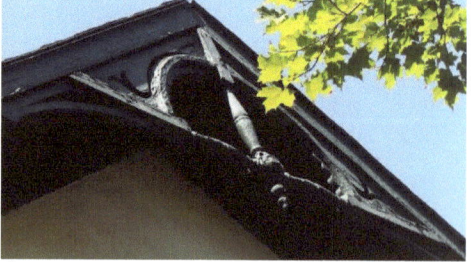

Within the peak is a decorative arch with spindle

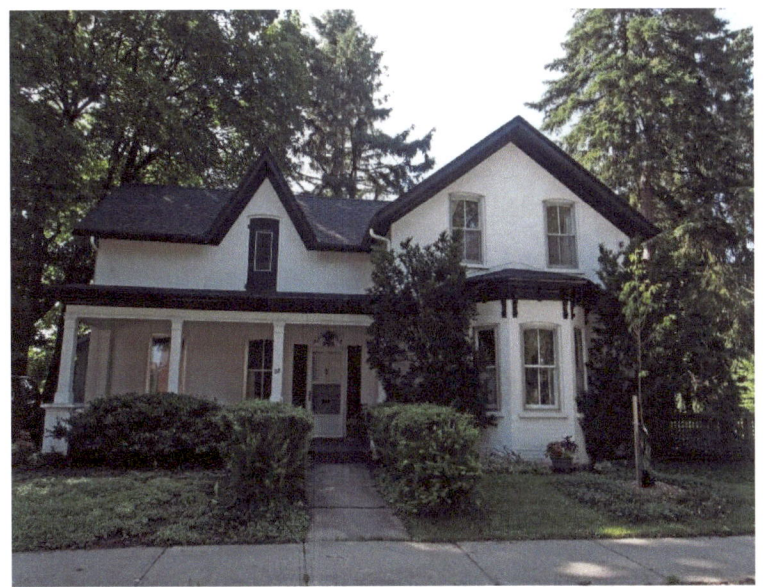

28 George Street – 1860 – Gothic style – arched windows

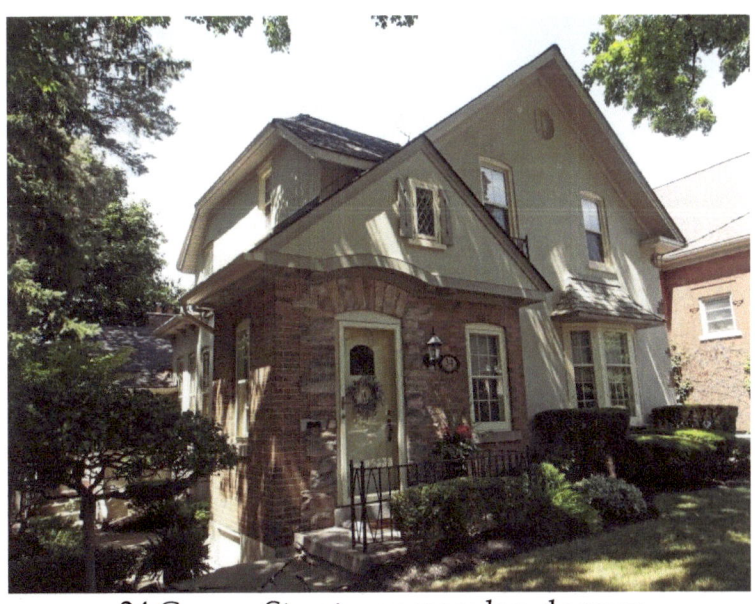

34 George Street – vernacular, dormer

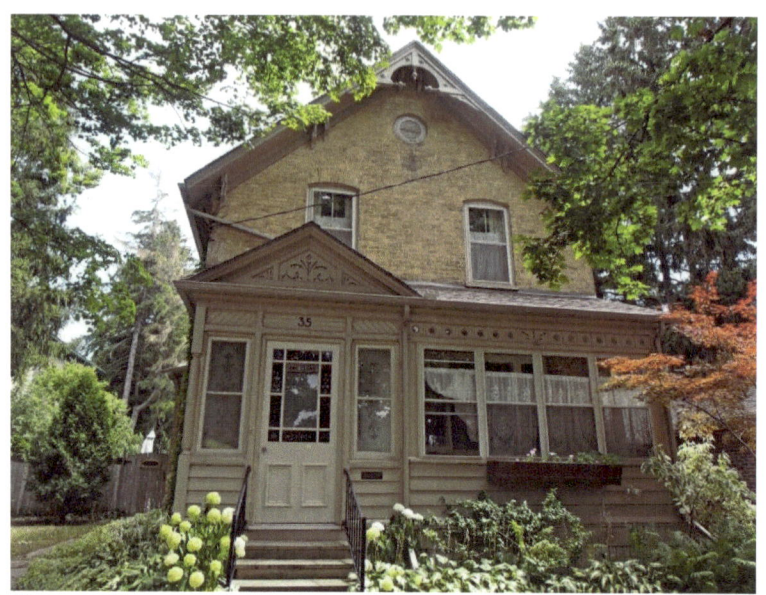

35 George Street – Gothic – pediment with decorated tympanum, within the peak is a decorative arch with spindle, brackets

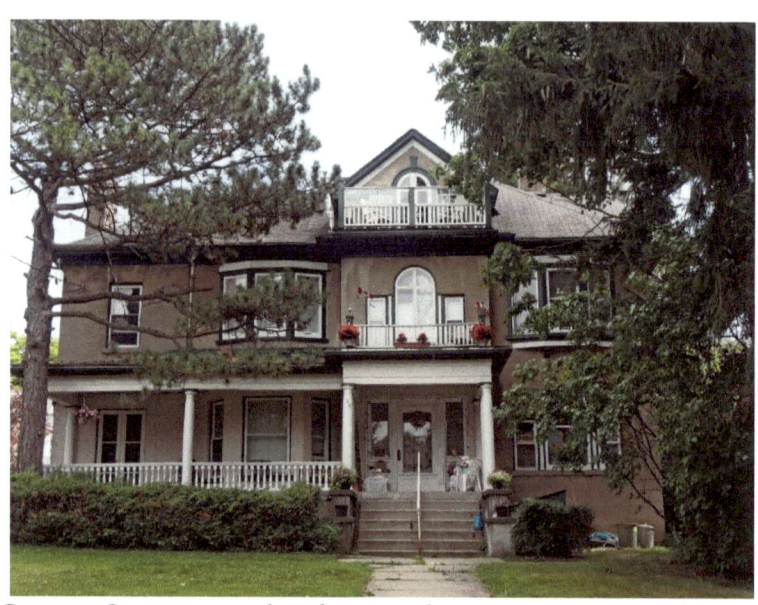

39 George Street – made of poured concrete – vernacular style – Palladian and bay windows – built 1903-1906 for Alfred Snyder owner of Snyder Brothers furniture

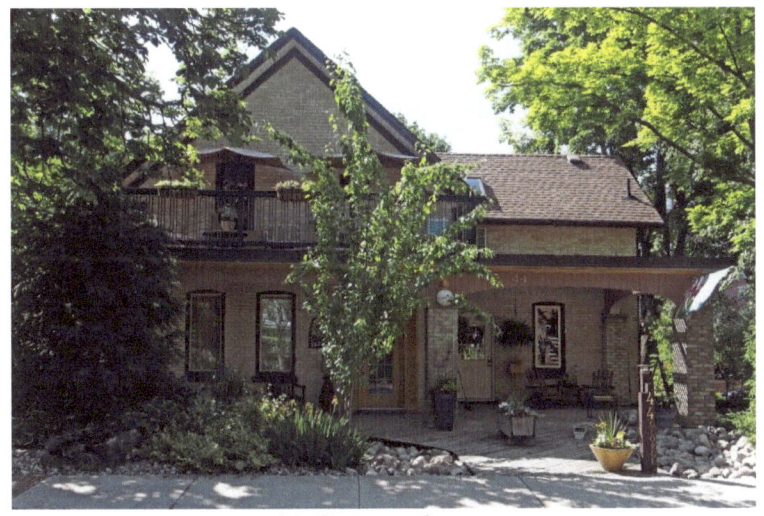

44 George Street

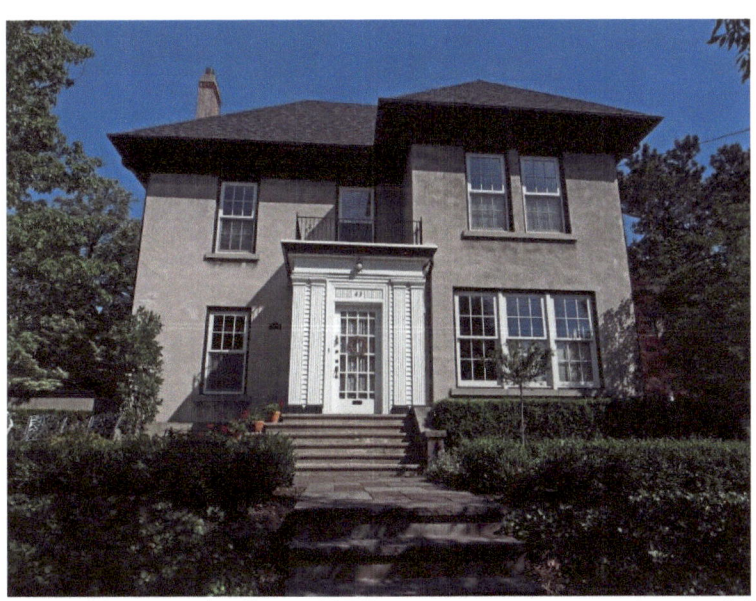

43 George Street – built in 1875 – note stucco exterior and front porch with embedded pillars, iron railing above porch

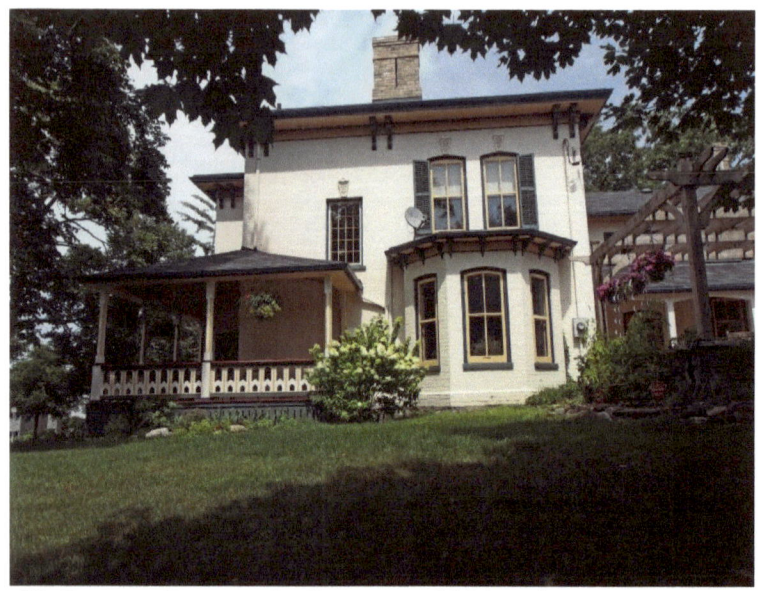

49 George Street – Italianate – 1886 – shutters, cornice brackets, keystones in arch above the windows

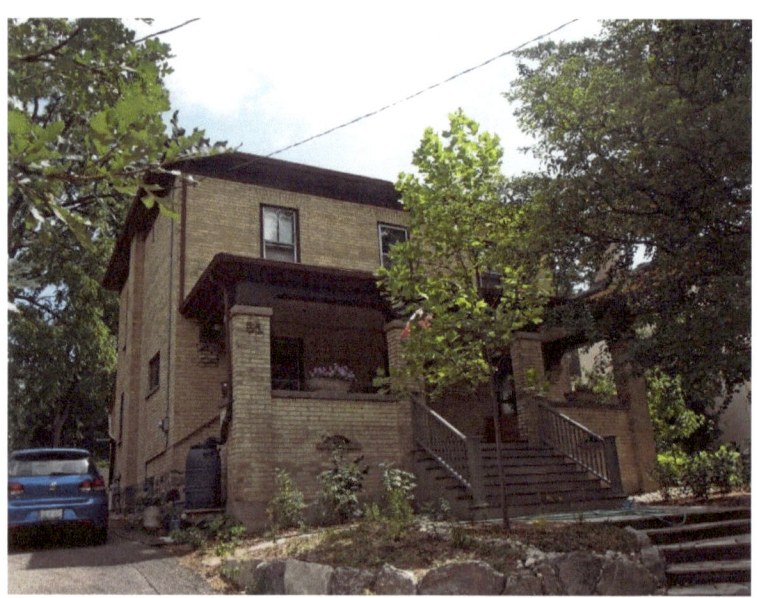

51 George Street - Italianate

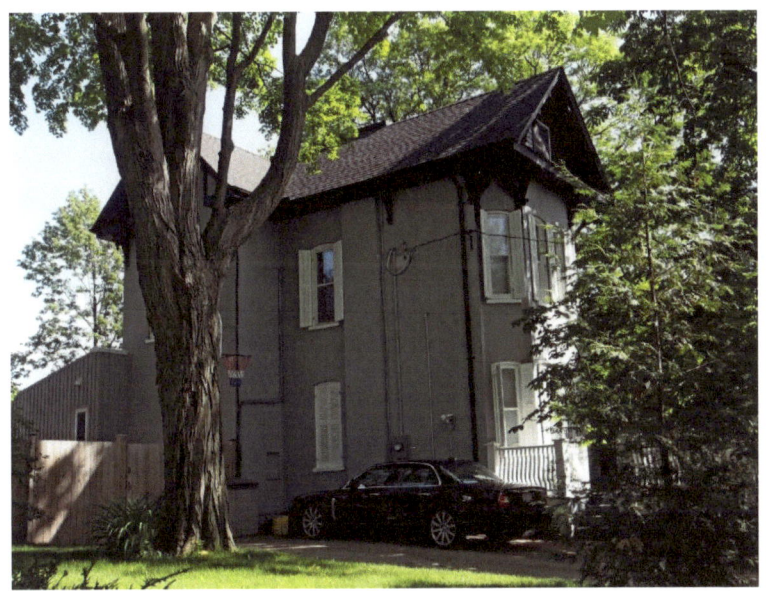

59 George Street – Edwardian, cornice brackets

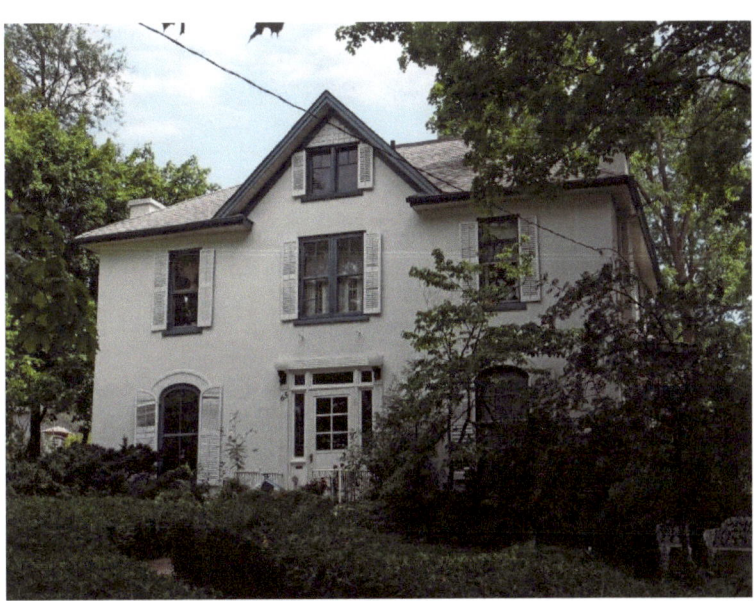

65 George Street – 1899 – stucco over red brick (three-brick thickness) – transom and sidelights around the front door

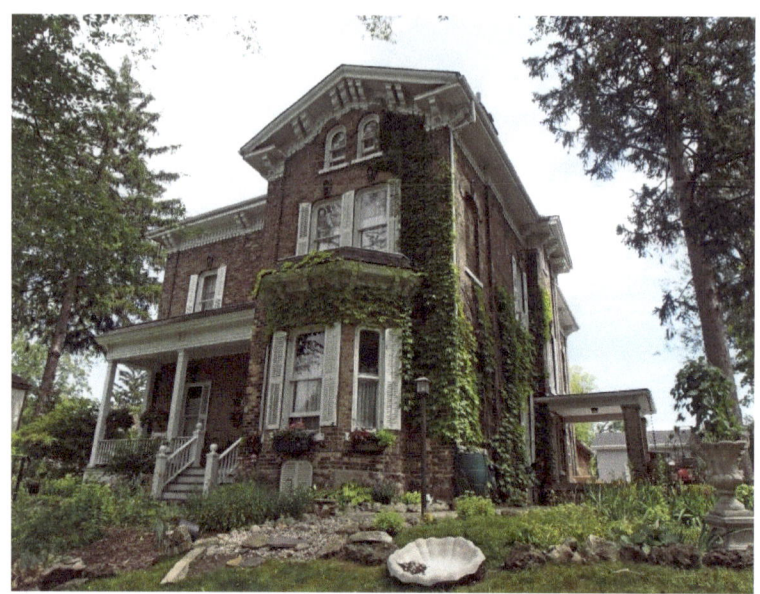

73 George Street – 1882 – Victorian style with Italianate details - fancy brackets under eaves, wood trim below the eaves, bay window; arched windows in the attic of the projecting bay; other windows have rounded corners; double front door; keystones over windows decorated with a motif consisting of a bunch of grapes

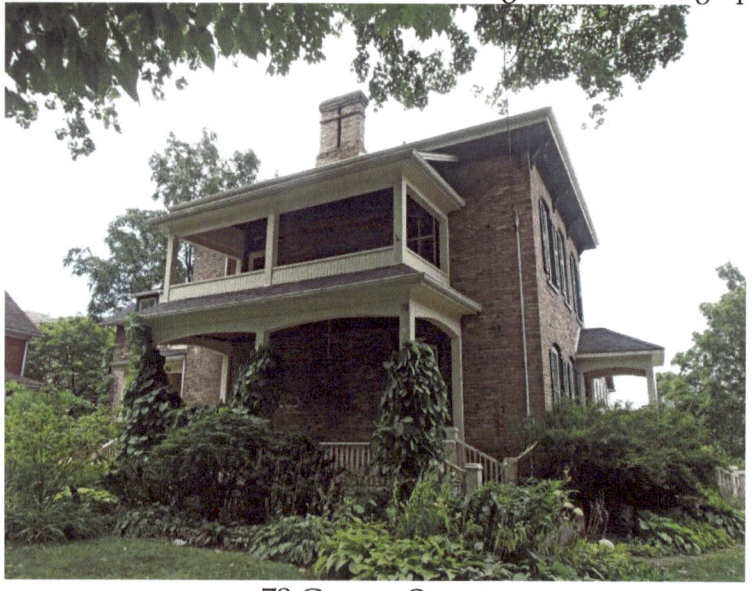

78 George Street

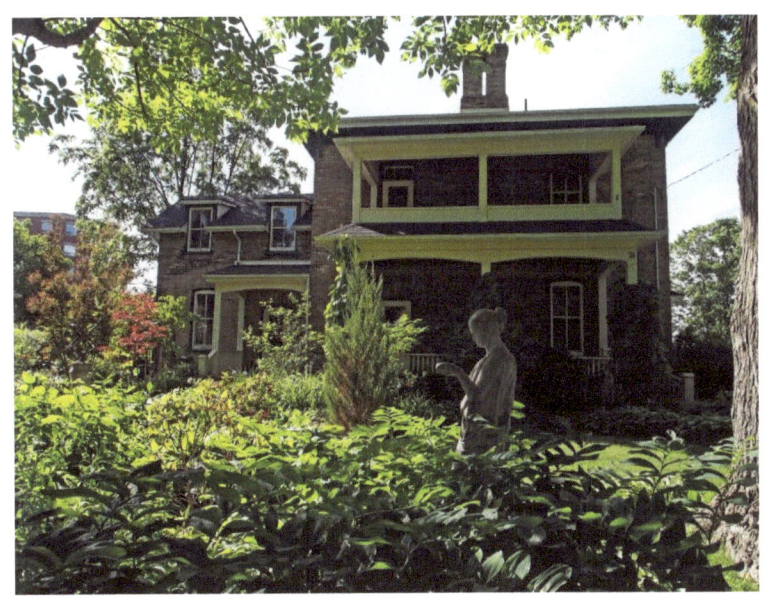

78 George Street – Italianate, 2-storey verandah

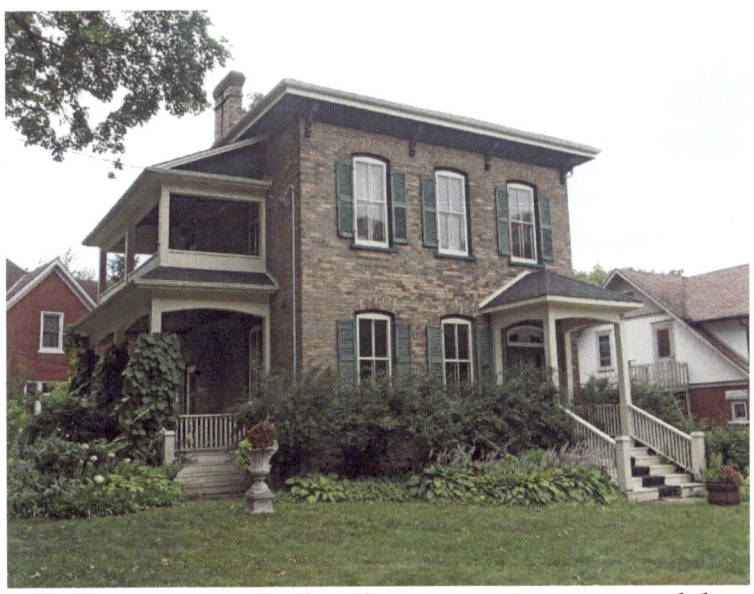

Italianate – cornice brackets, two-storey verandah

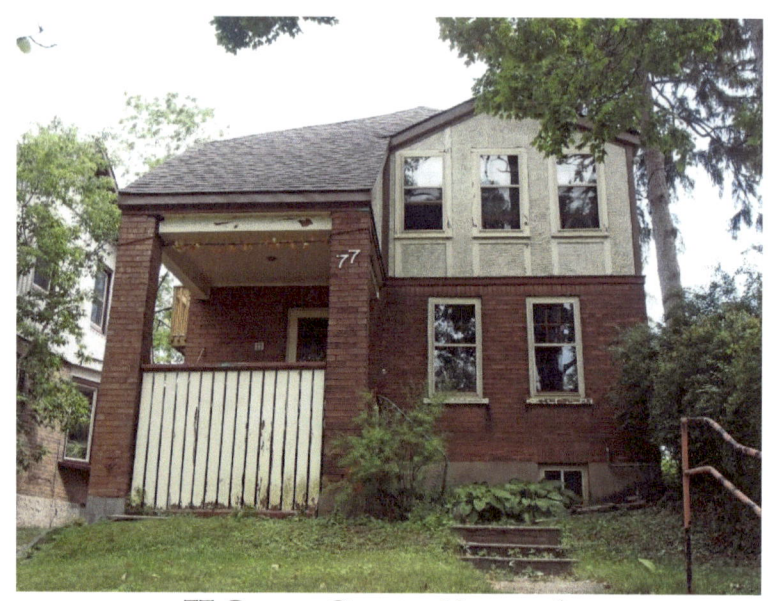

77 George Street – Vernacular

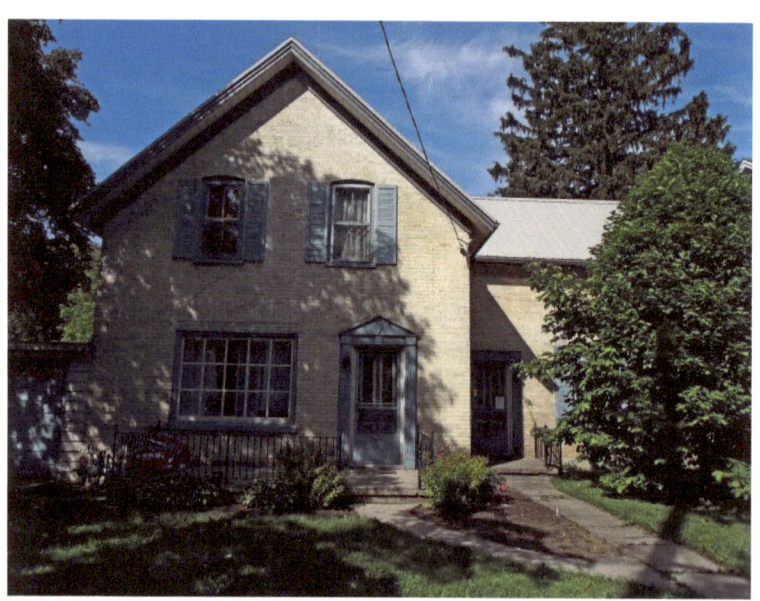

50 Willow Street - Gothic

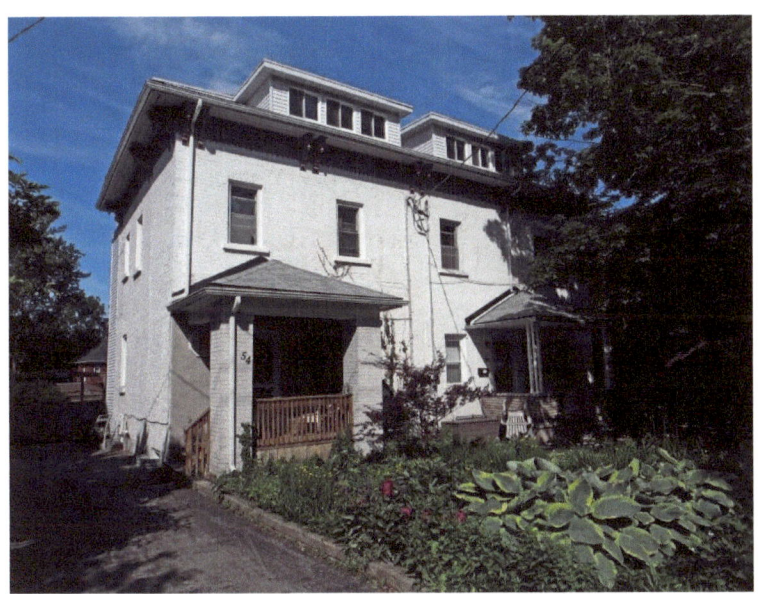

54-56 Willow Street – 1889 – fancy wood trim under the eaves, paired cornice brackets, dormers in attic

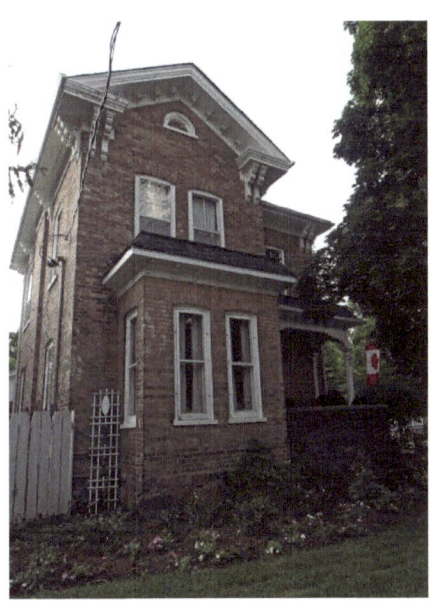

78 Willow Street – cornice brackets, fancy brackets under eaves, rectangular bay window

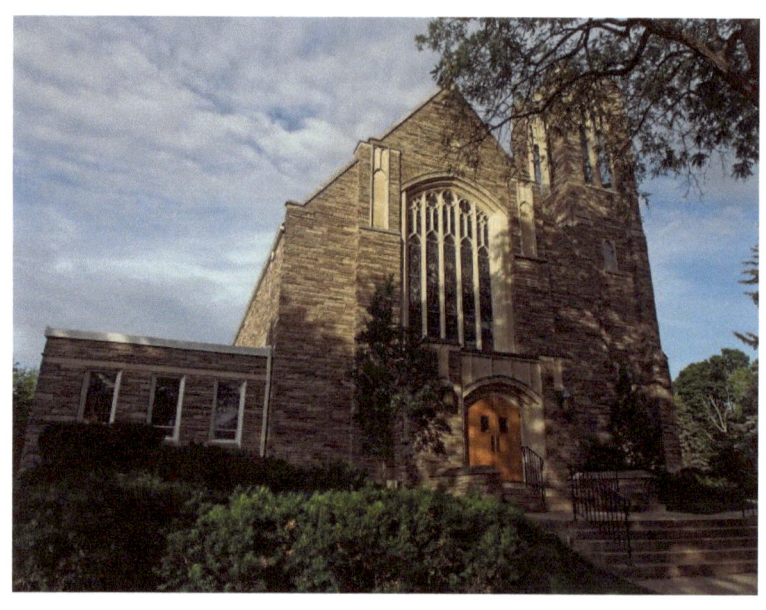

22 Willow Street – St. John's Lutheran Church – Gothic,
3-storey bell tower

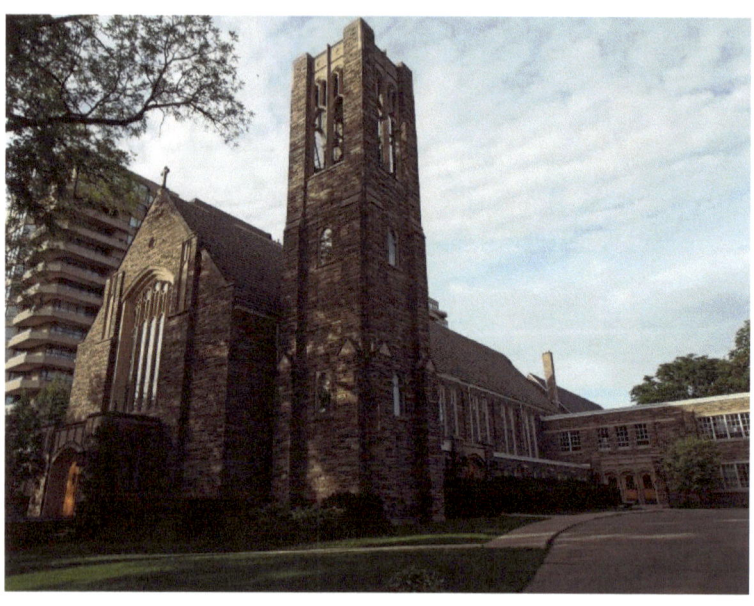

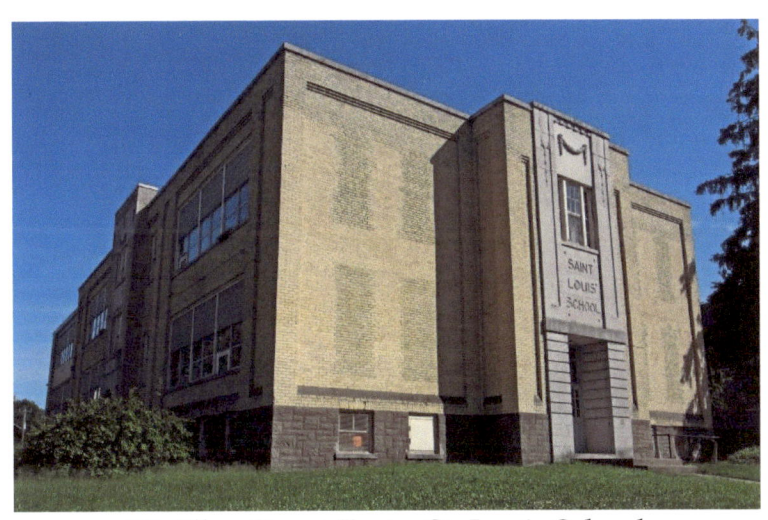

75 Allen Street East – St. Louis School

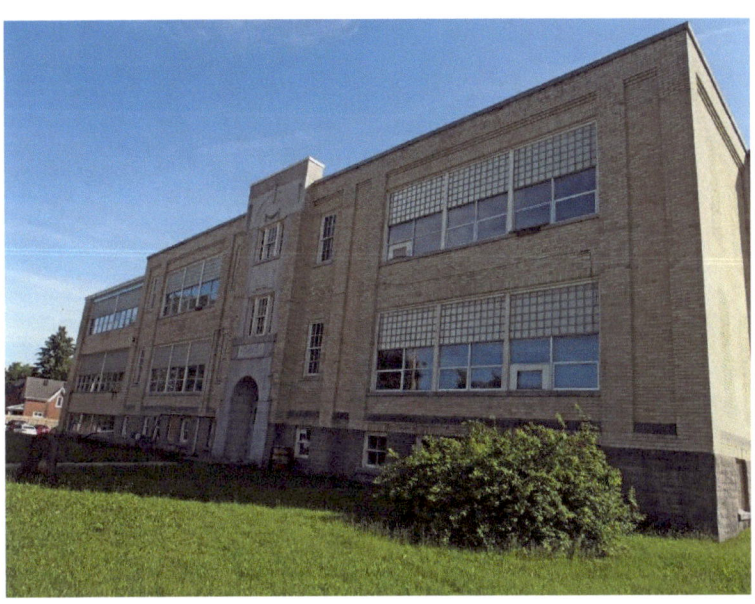

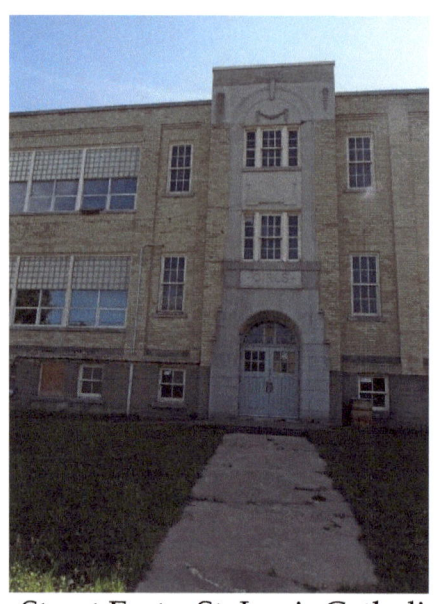

75 Allen Street East – St. Louis Catholic School
Vernacular Beaux Arts style – 1905

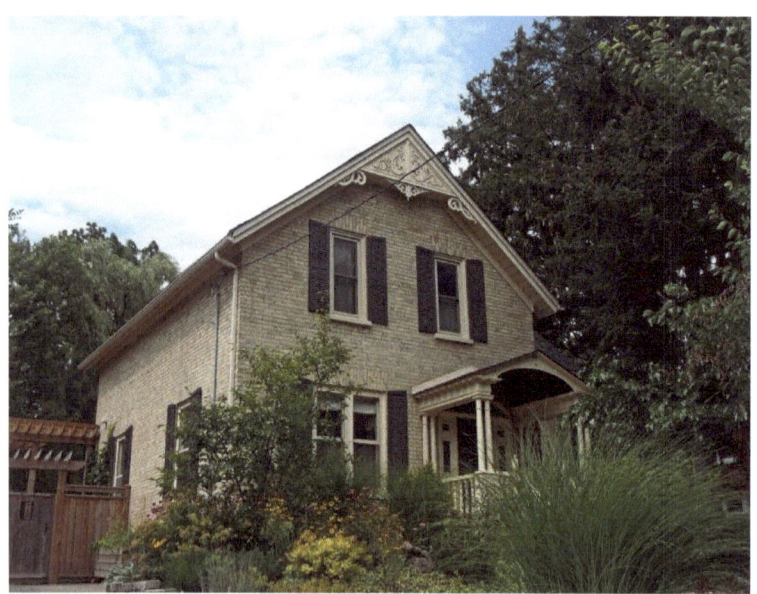

64 Allen Street East – Gothic – decorative bargeboard in arch

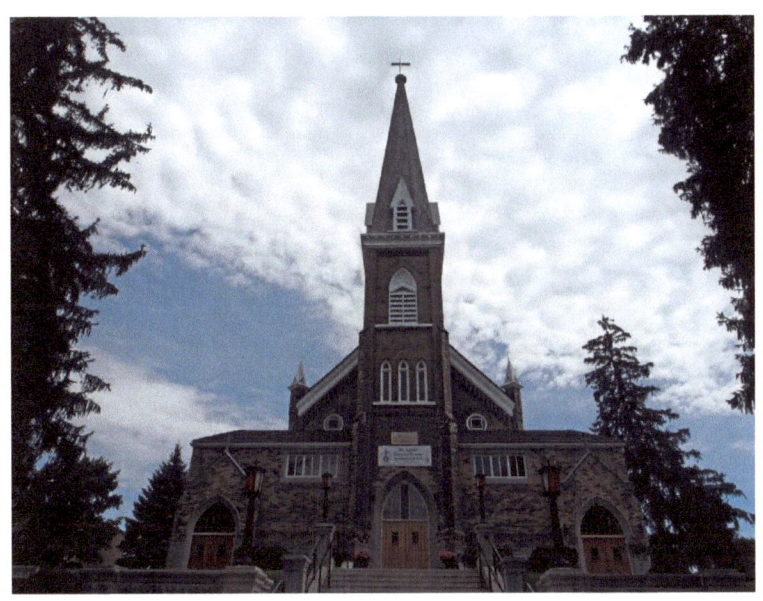

53 Allen Street East – St. Louis Catholic Church – 1890
Lancet windows in bell tower with spire,
bevelled dentil moulding under eaves

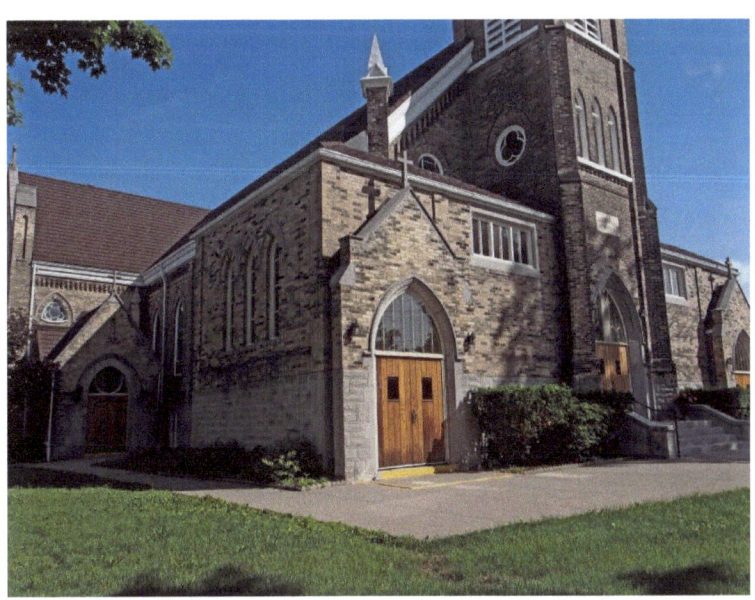

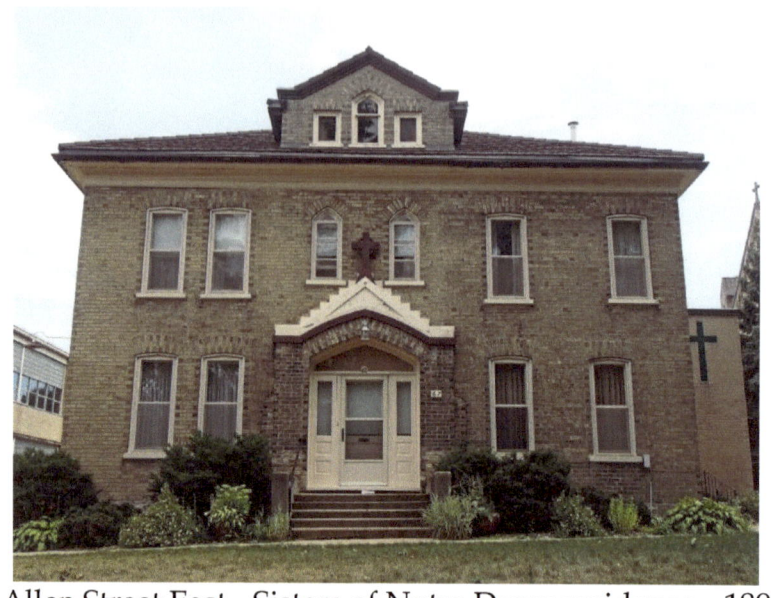

67 Allen Street East - Sisters of Notre Dame residence – 1895 –
Palladian window in dormer – Georgian style

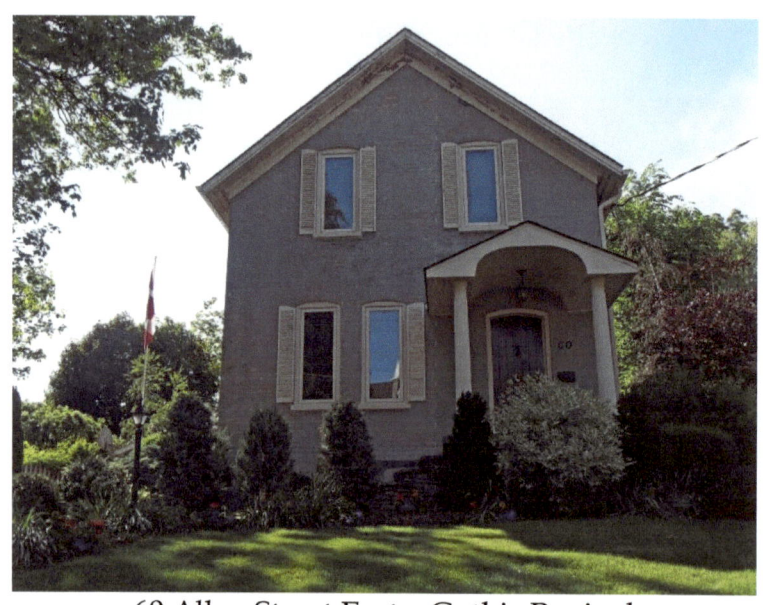

60 Allen Street East – Gothic Revival

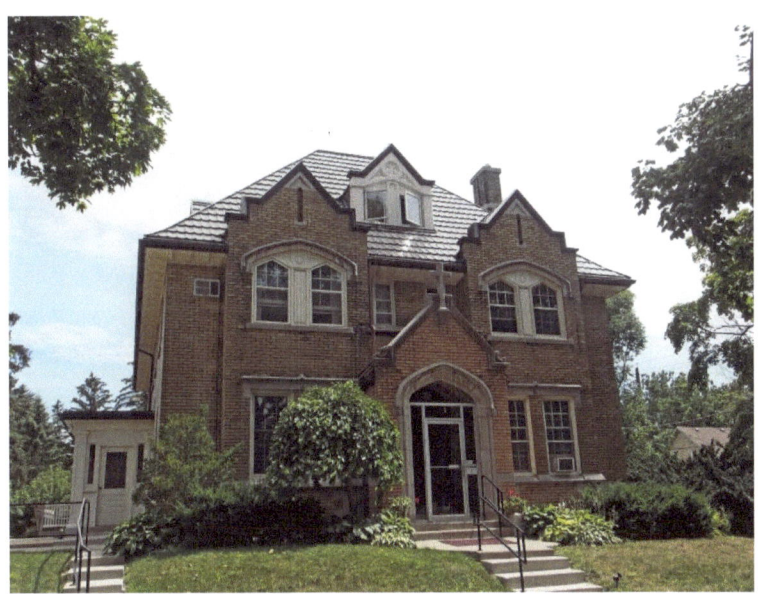

53 Allen Street East – new rectory – 1928 – Period Revival Style – medieval influences – the gables have loopholes, found in medieval architecture as a place for launching arrows

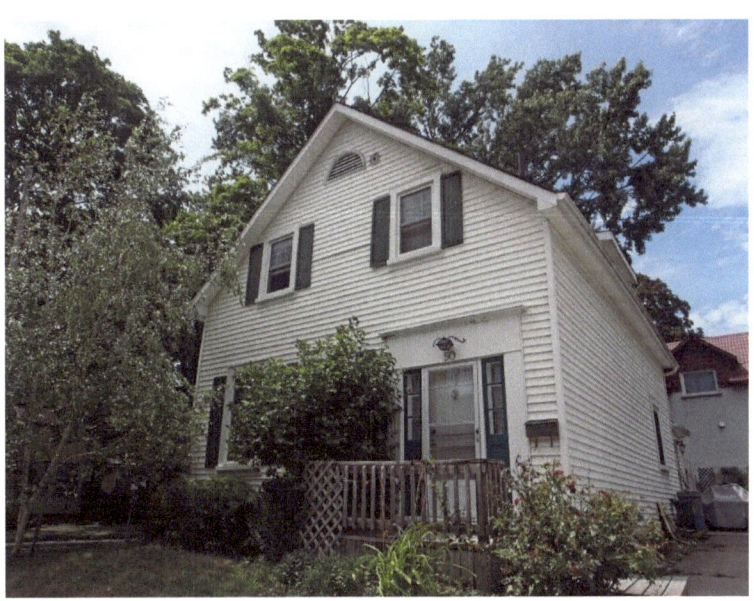

50 Allen Street East – Gothic Revival

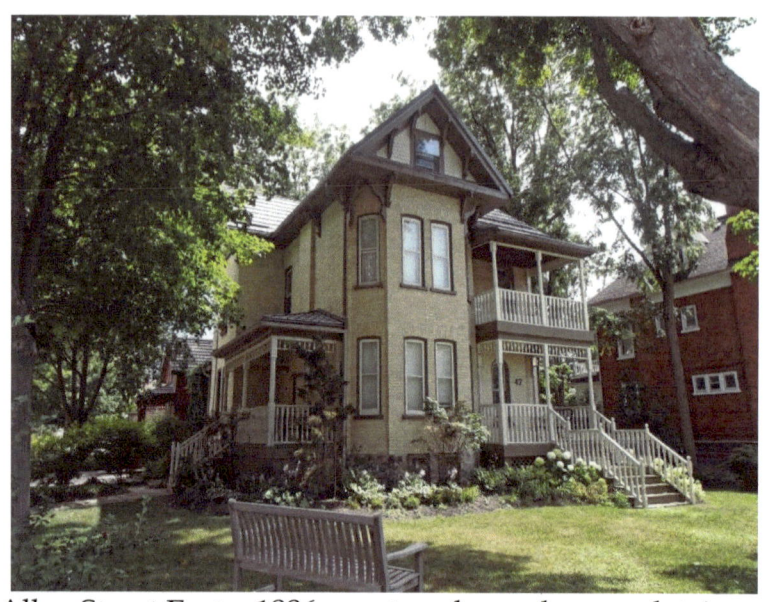

47 Allen Street East – 1886 – restored wooden porch trim with turned spindles

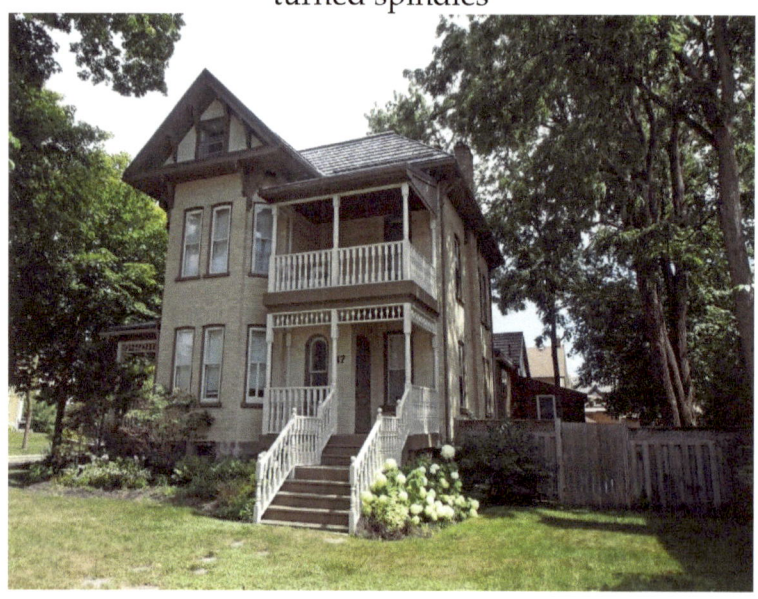

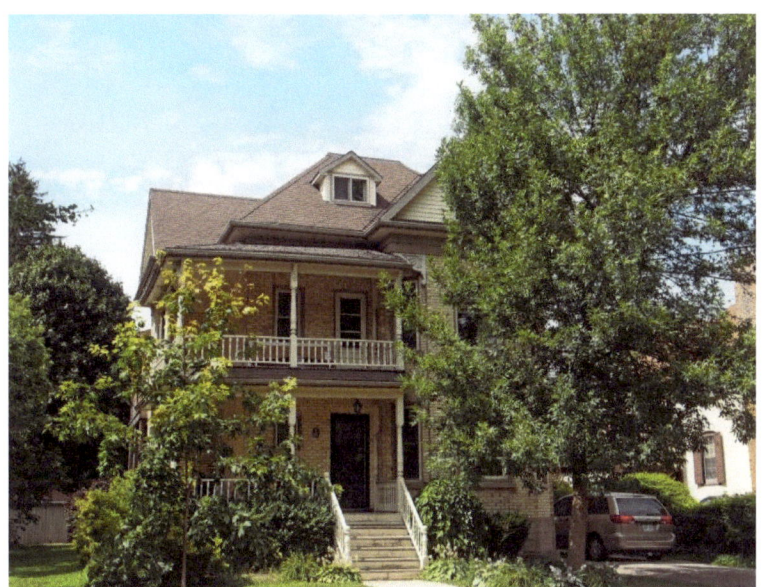

42 Allen Street East

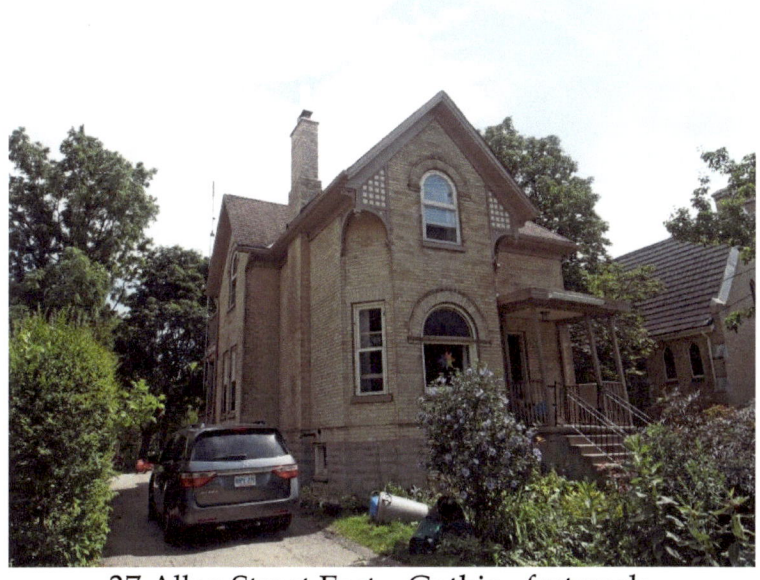

37 Allen Street East – Gothic - fretwork,
Romanesque style window arch

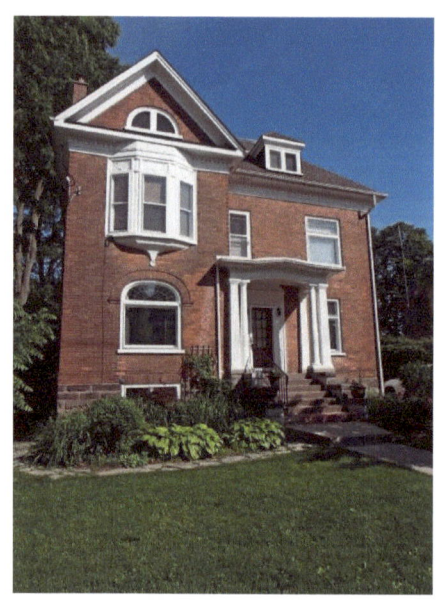

41 Allen Street East – Edwardian, oriel window, dormer

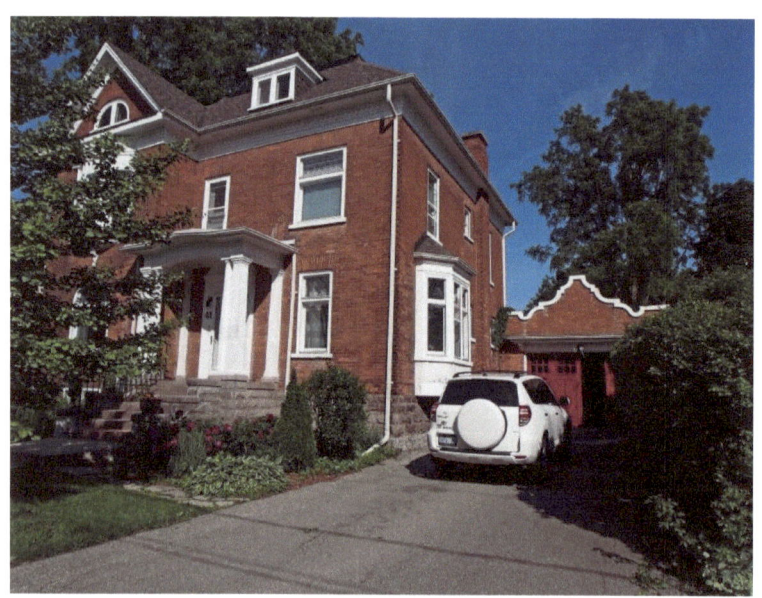

Bay window on side; original decorative garage

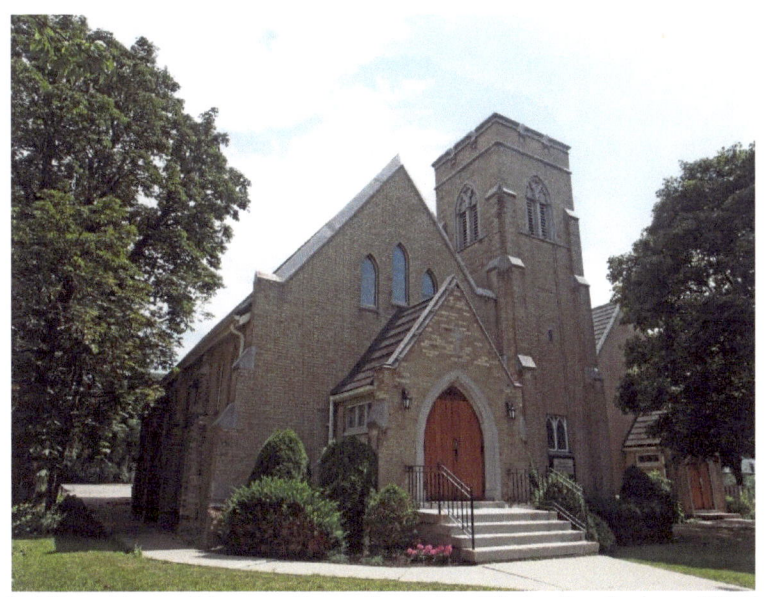

33 Allen Street East – Church of the Holy Saviour – 1897 –
square Roman tower

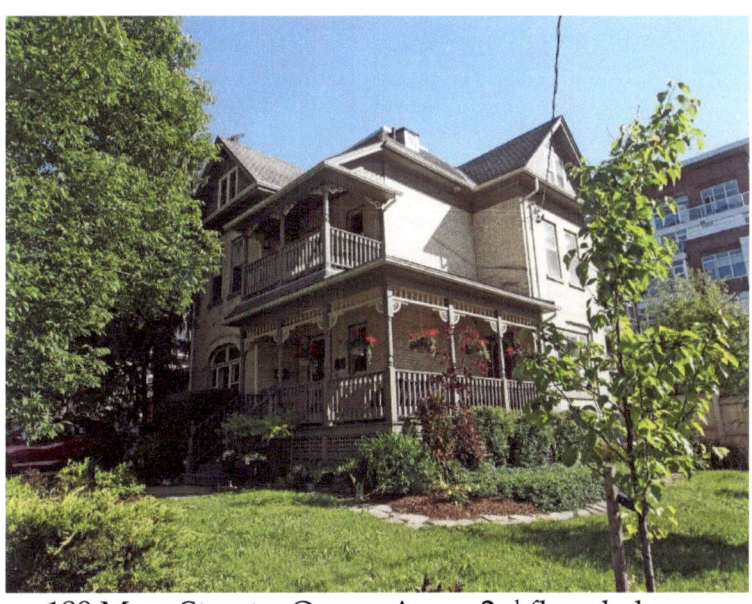

189 Mary Street – Queen Anne, 2nd floor balcony

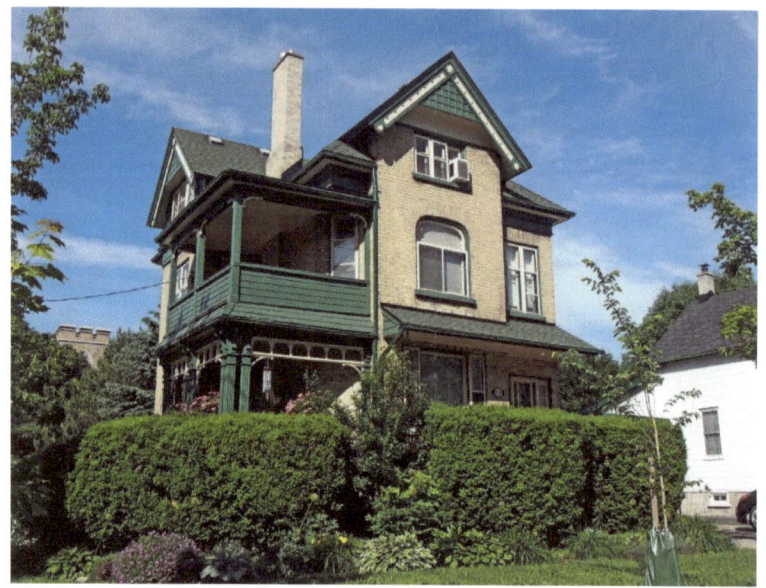

190 Mary Street – Queen Anne style, 2-storey verandah

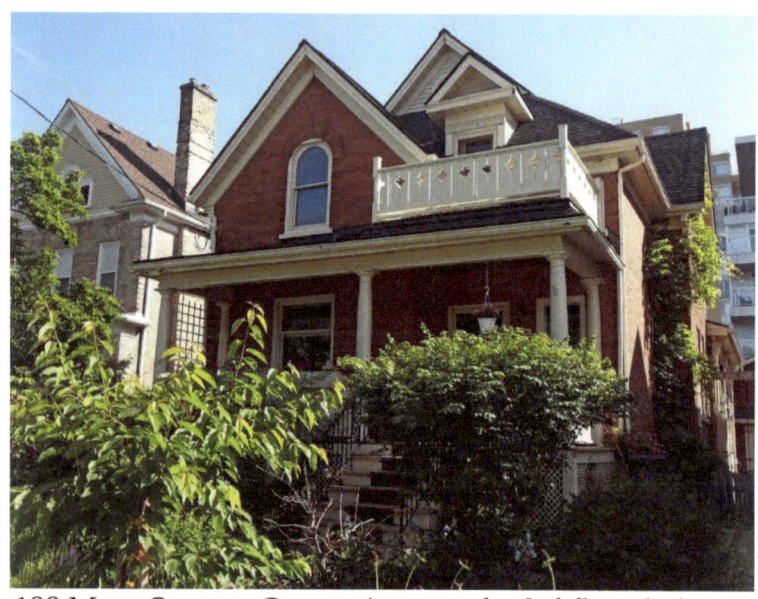

199 Mary Street – Queen Anne style, 2nd floor balcony

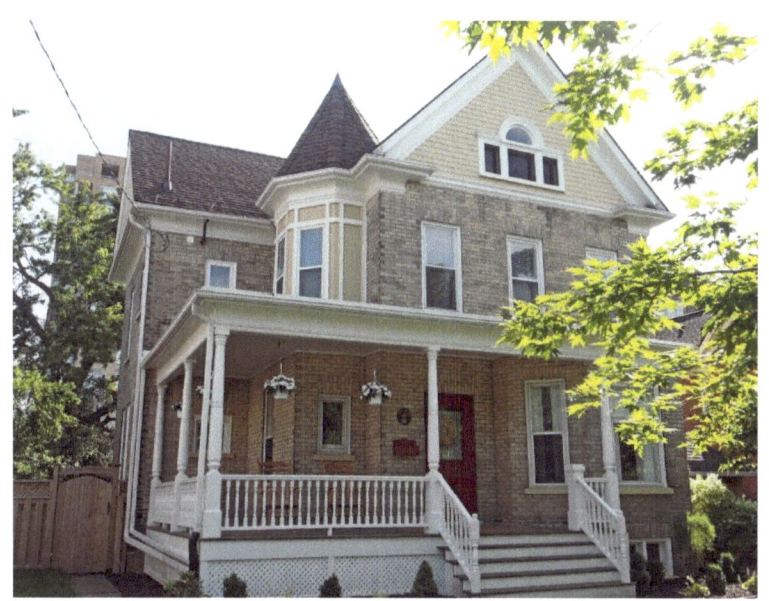

203 Mary Street – Queen Anne – turret, Palladian window

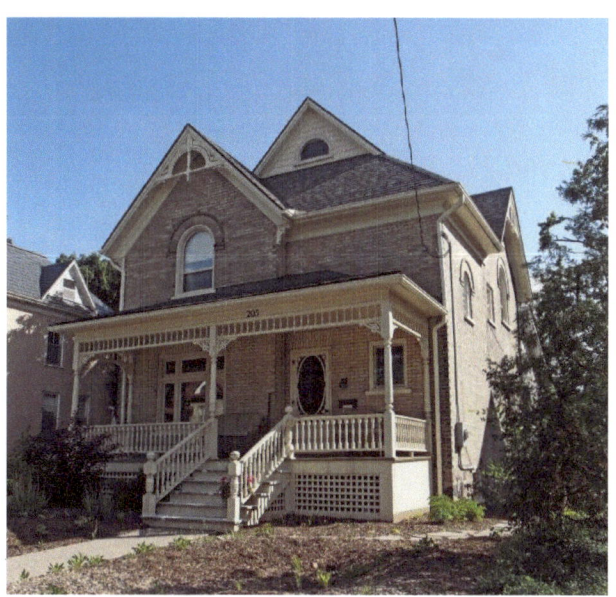

205 Mary Street - within each of the peaks is a decorative arch
with spindle and applied scrollwork,
wood-turned verandah roof supports

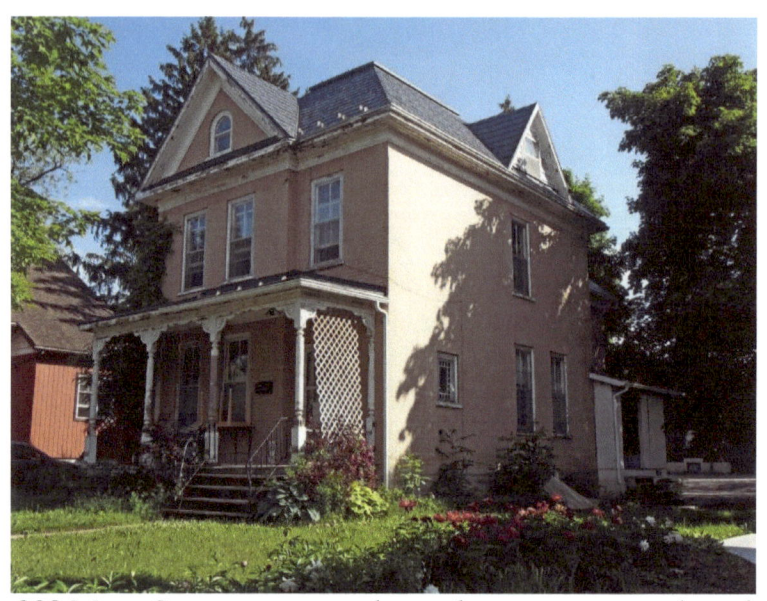

209 Mary Street – vernacular – almost a mansard roof
wood-turned verandah roof supports

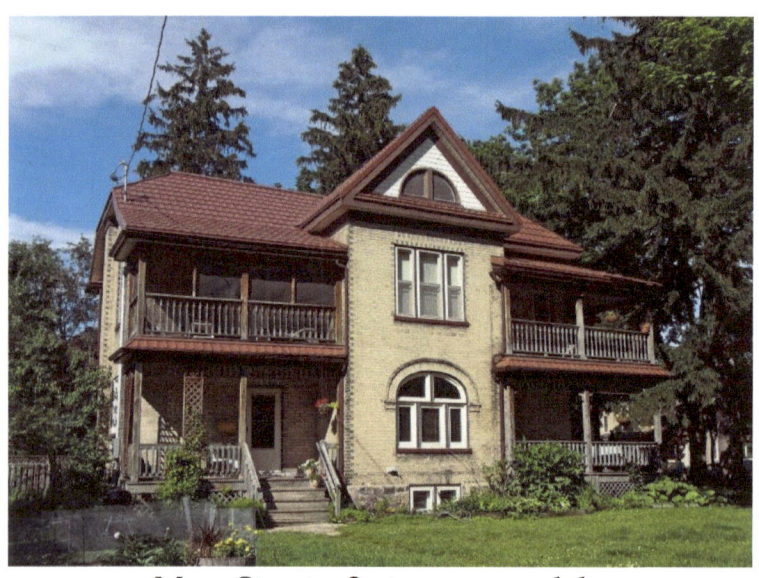

Mary Street – 2-storey verandah,
Romanesque style window arch,

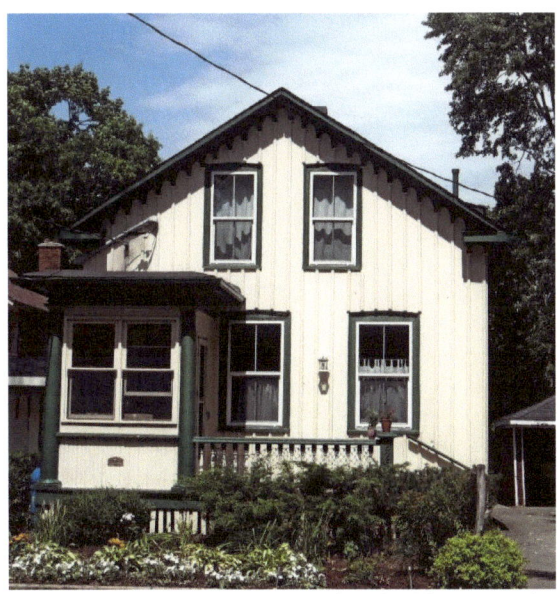

222 Mary Street – 1859 - one-and-a-half storey board and batten house, the battens are individually moulded and topped by capitals connected by arches; cornice return on front gable; 2-over-2 window panes; entrance portico supported by two Doric columns – now enclosed

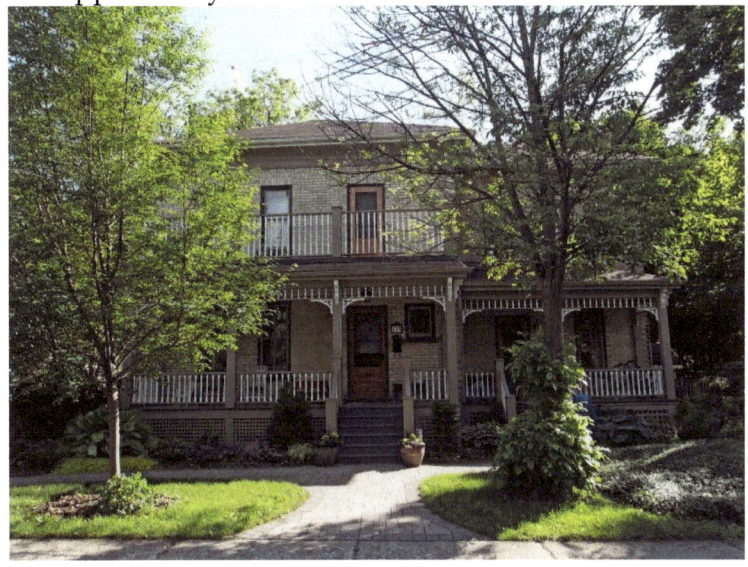

227 Mary Street

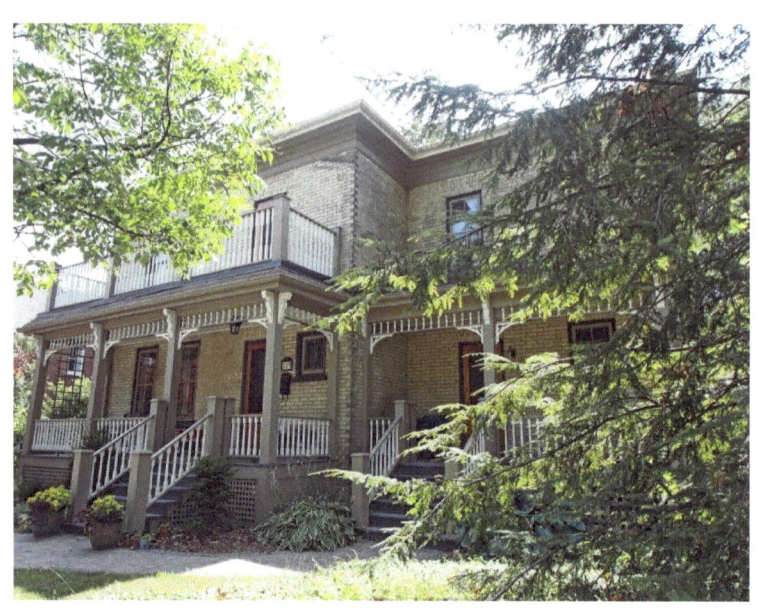

227 Mary Street – Italianate - two-storey verandah

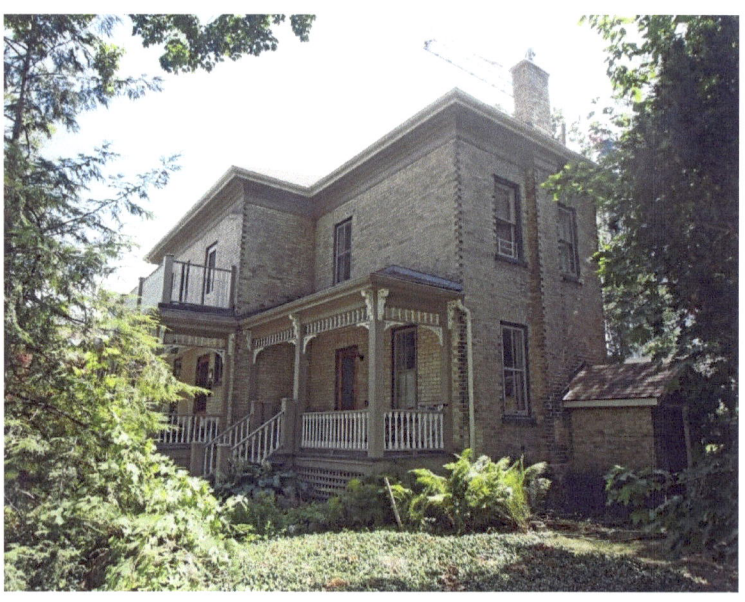

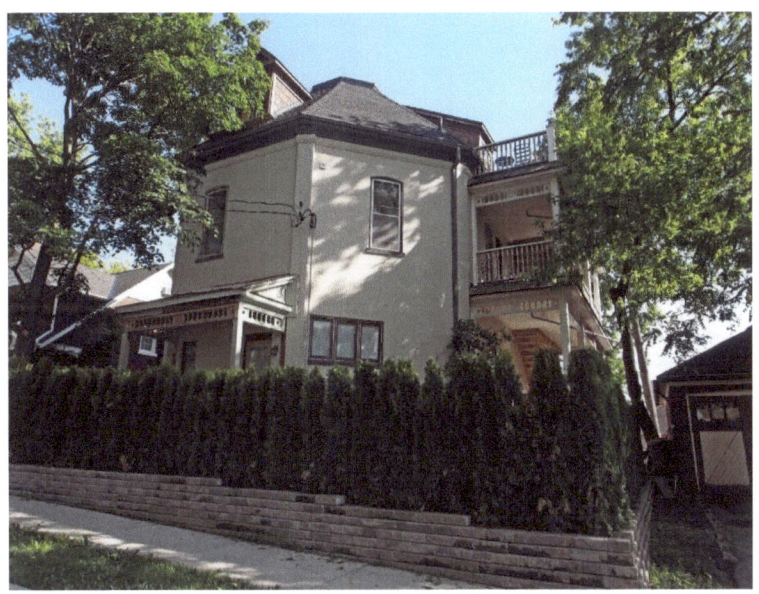

Mary Street

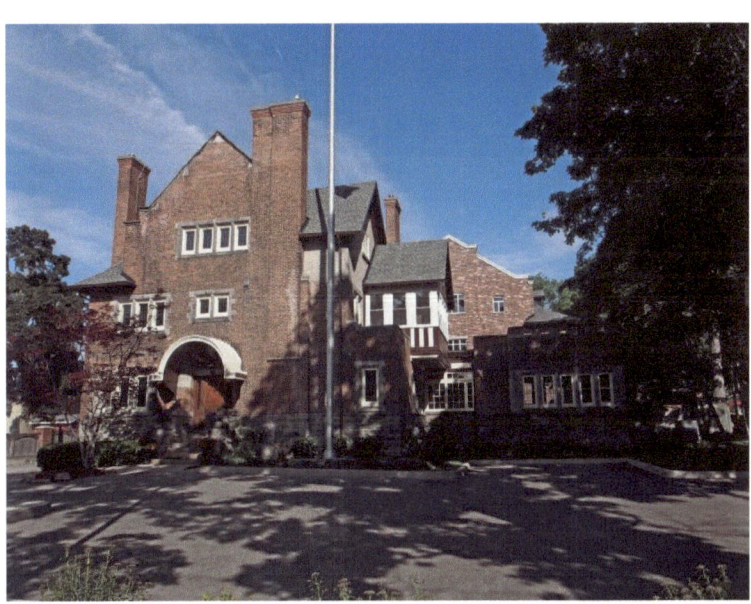

31 Union Street East – English Manor House – 1913 – 2 storey
red brick with 1 storey wing – 8200 square foot Seagram Bauer
house was built for Thomas Seagram, son of distilling
magnate Joseph Seagram

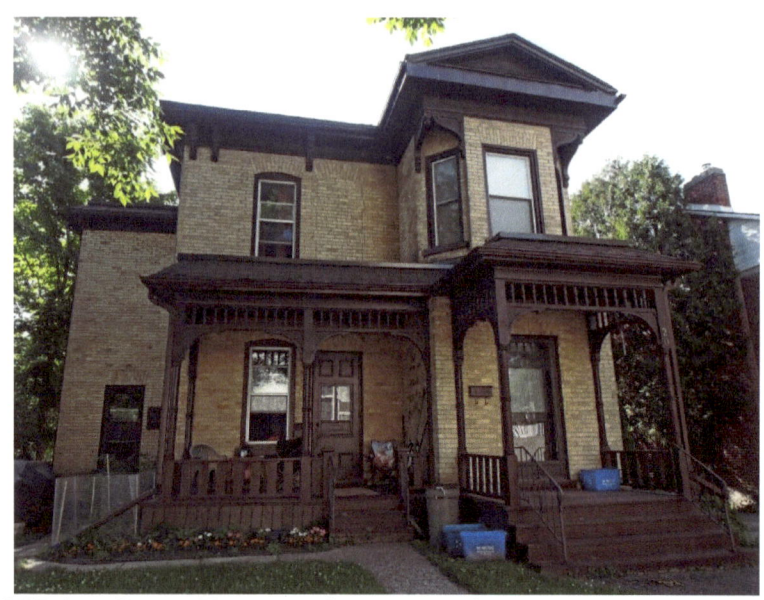

20 Union Street East – Italianate with two-storey projecting bay topped with a pediment; cornice brackets and fretwork

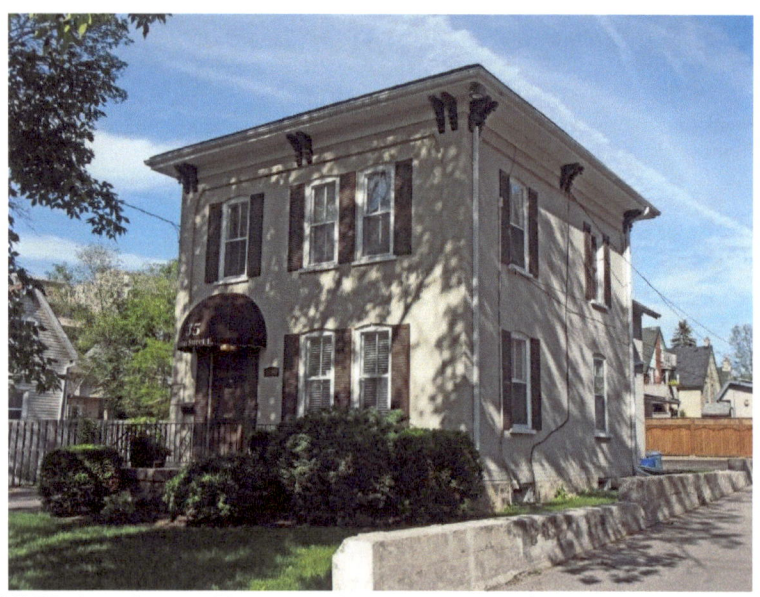

35 Union Street East – Italianate, paired cornice brackets

Brubacher House

The Brubacher family was of Swiss-Mennonite background; their ancestors came from Europe to the United States after facing persecution during the Radical Reformation. In 1803, they moved with twenty-five Mennonite families from Lancaster County, Pennsylvania to this area. John Brubacher Sr. got married and had a family. His son John E. Brubacher was raised in downtown Kitchener, and married Magdalena Musselman in 1846. Four years later, their permanent home in Waterloo was built in the Pennsylvania German style of architecture.

John and Magdalena had fourteen children in this home, thirteen of whom lived until adulthood. Their farm was mostly orchards. The main floor has four rooms, the winter kitchen, the pantry, the bedroom, and the parlor. Upstairs there were bedrooms for the children. Downstairs, the family had a Summer Kitchen for the warmer months. The walkout basement made it easy for them to come and go as needed.

The winter kitchen was the heart of the home. Meals were prepared and eaten, and homework and other chores were carried out here. The interior reflects a Pennsylvania German Mennonite home of the 1850-90 periods. The furnishings are an authentic reflection the time period. There is a fireplace, china cupboard with wedding china, and a farmer's couch. The pantry was used for storage and minor food preparations, as well as being the main washroom. The bedroom was where the parents slept with any infants who needed the main fireplace for heat through the night. The mattress was of straw and placed on a rope bed. The parlor was only used on Sundays or during special events like weddings or funerals.

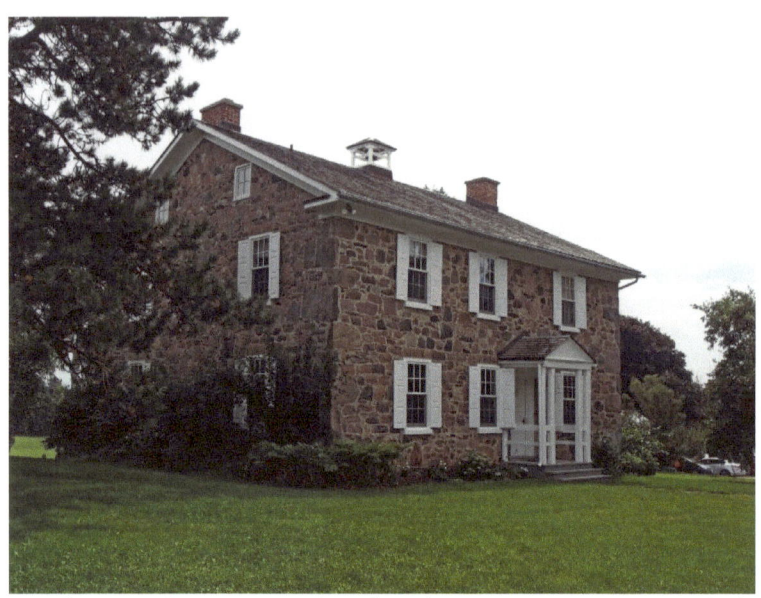

Pennsylvania German style of architecture - steep roof, thick walls and small, irregularly spaced windows, three-room layout with large kitchen on one side of the central chimney, and two smaller rooms (parlor and bedroom) on the other side

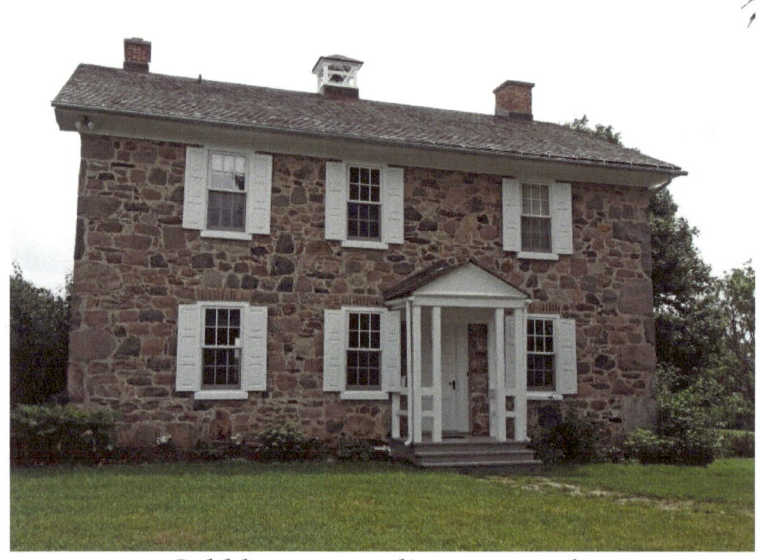

Cobblestone, pediment, cupola

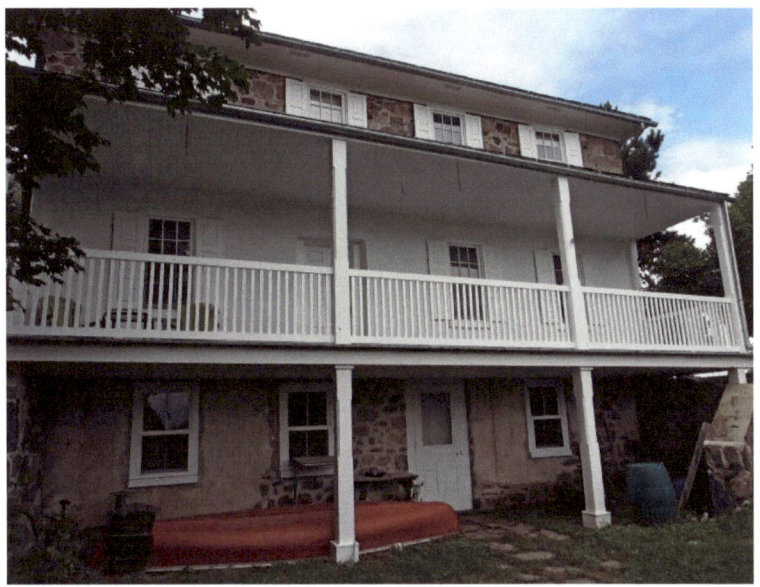

Walkout basement where summer kitchen was located with verandah above

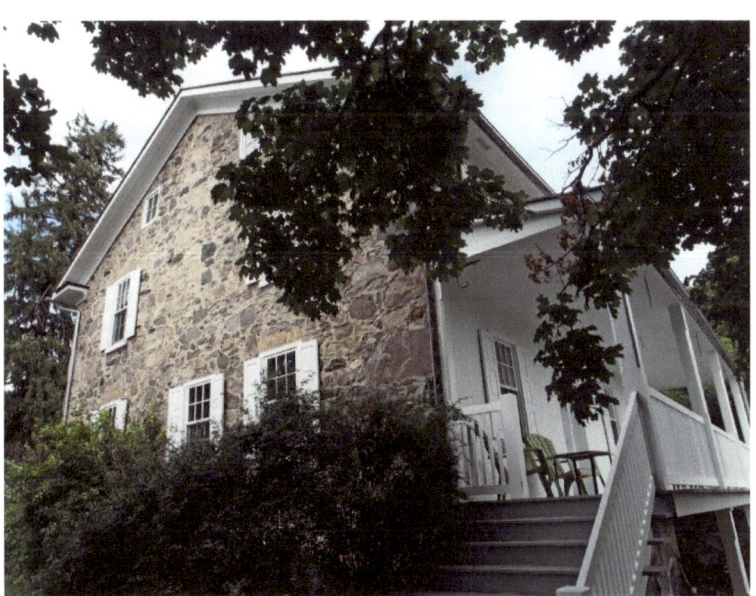

Cornice return on gable

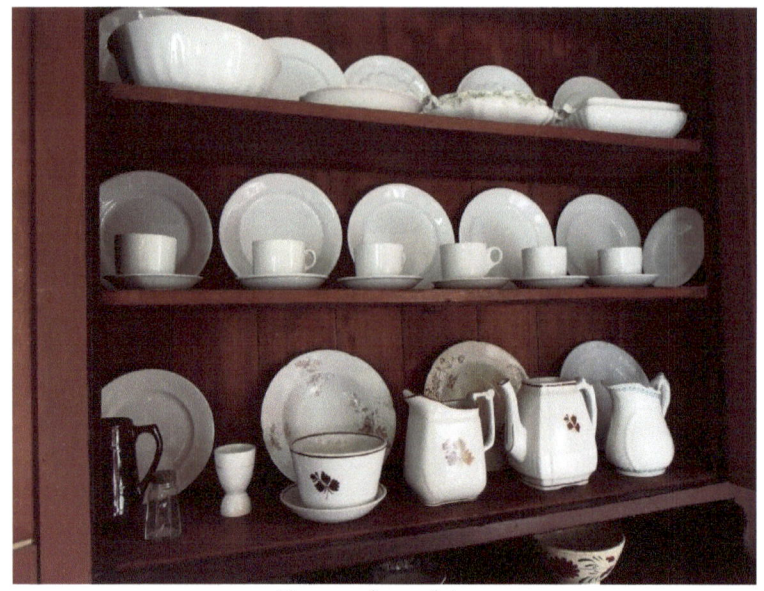

Everyday china

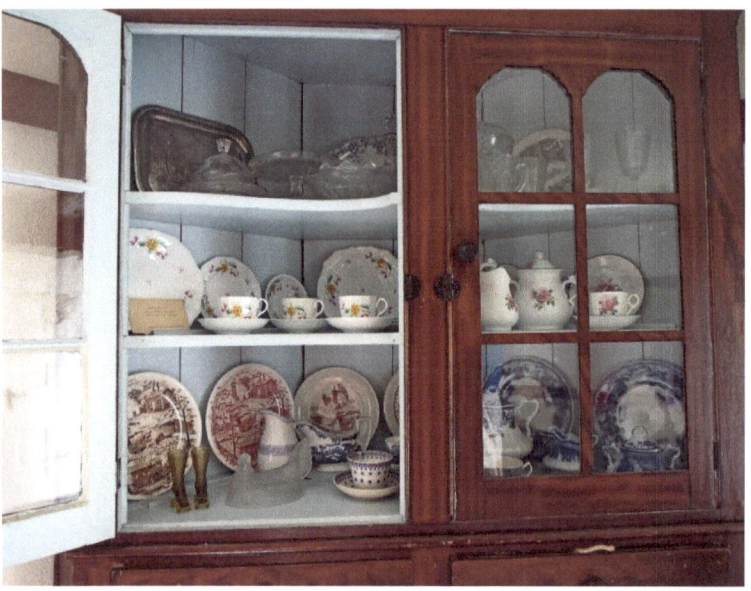

Special china

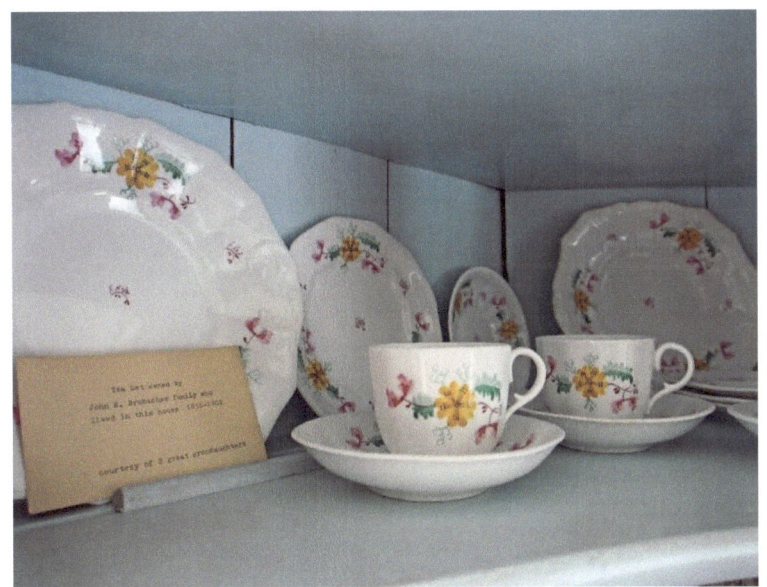

Tea set owned by John E. Brubacher family who lived in the house from 1850-1902

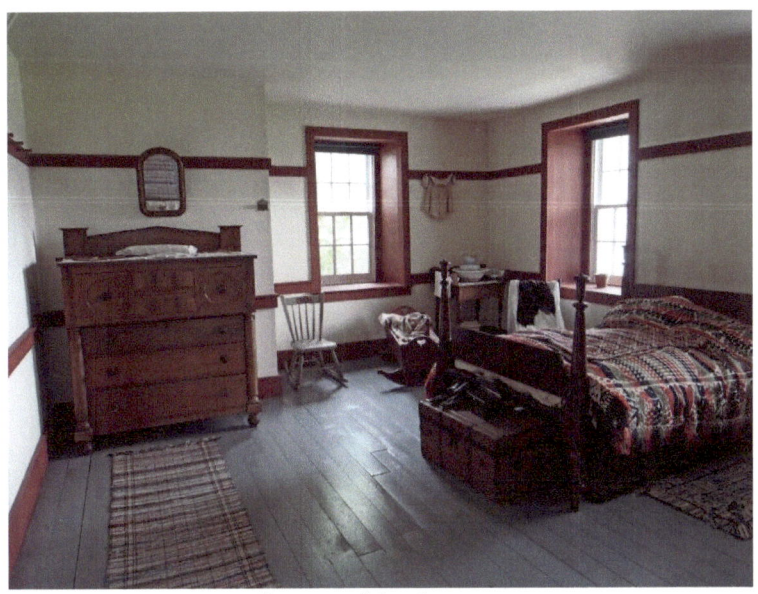

Parents' bedroom

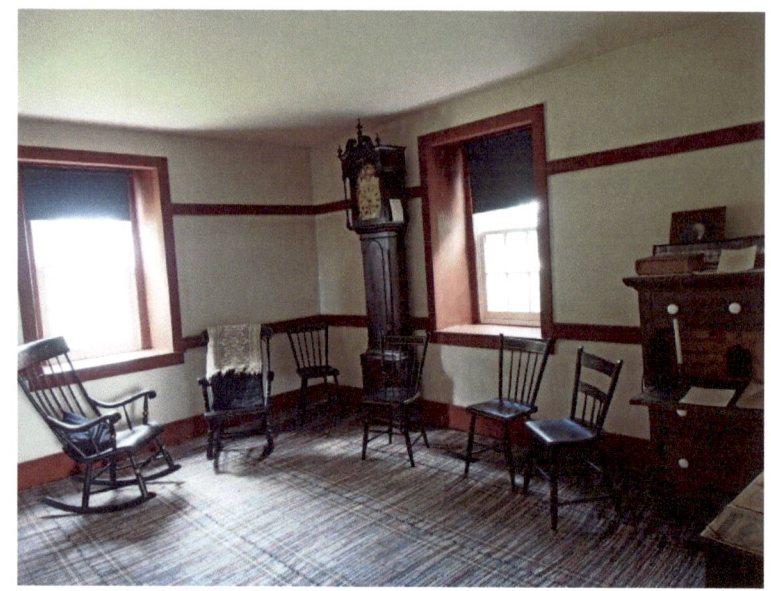

Parlor

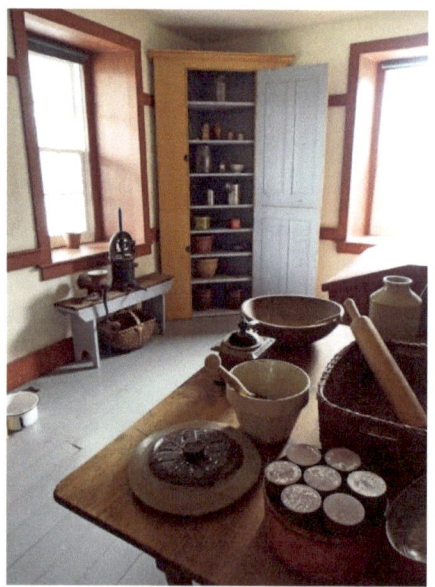

Pantry

Architectural Terms

Bay Window: A window that projects out from a wall, in a semicircular, rectangular, or polygonal design. Used frequently in Gothic and Victorian designs. Example: 88 William Street West, Page 9	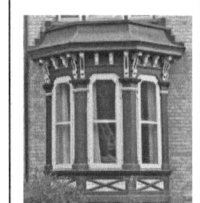
Brackets: a decorative or weight-bearing structural element which forms a right angle with one side against a wall and the other under a projecting surface such as an eave or roof. Example: 54-56 Willow Street, see Page 35	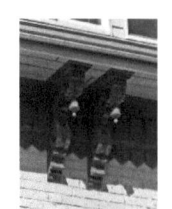
Buttress: a masonry structure built against or projecting from a wall which serves to support or reinforce the wall. In Canadian architecture, they are sometimes used for decoration. Example: 15 George Street, see Page 24	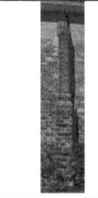
Cobblestone architecture: Refers to the use of cobblestones embedded in mortar as a method for erecting walls on houses and commercial buildings. Example: Brubacher House, Page 54	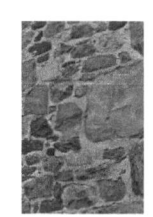
Cornice: originally the wooden overhang of the roof. With the use of stone, brick, iron and steel, the cornice is any projecting shelf at the top of a ceiling or roof. They can be very decorative. Example: 73 George Street, Page 32	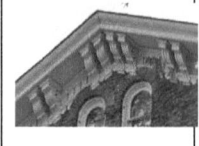

Cornice Return: decorative element on the end of a gable. Example: 171 King Street South, Page 13	
Dentil Moulding: an even series of rectangles used as ornamental decoration in cornices. Example: William Street East, see Page 9	
Dormer: (French for "sleep") a gable end window that pierces through the plane of a sloping roof surface to create usable space in the top floor or attic of a building by adding headroom. Example: 215 King Street South, see Page 20	
Fretwork: interlaced decorative design resembling a bracket Example: 20 Union Street East, Page 52	
Gable: the triangular portion of a wall between the edges of a sloping roof. Example: 88 William Street, Page 9	
Keystones and Voussoirs: a voussoir is a wedge-shaped element used in building an arch. A keystone is the central stone that locks all the stones into position, allowing the arch to bear weight. A keystone is often enlarged and embellished. Example: 73 George Street, Page 32	

Lancet Window: a tall, narrow window with a pointed arch at its top. Example: 15 George Street, see Page 24	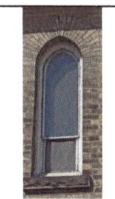
Mansard Roof: This style was popularized by Francois Mansart (1598-1666), an accomplished architect of the French Baroque period and especially fashionable during the Second French Empire (1852-1870). This roof is almost flat on the top section, with two slopes on each of its sides with the lower slope at a steeper angle than the upper and having dormer windows. Example: 209 Mary Street – vernacular roof, Page 48	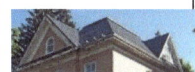
Oriel Window: These small areas were originally set into walls and galleries for the purpose of private prayer. Over time, any projecting window or area on an upper floor was called an oriel. Example: 41 Allen Street East, Page 44	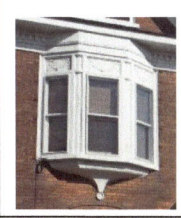
Palladian Window: a large window that is divided into three sections with the centre section larger than the two side sections and usually arched. Example: 203 Mary Street, Page 47	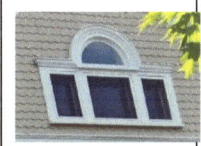
Pediment: a triangular section above the horizontal structure (entablature), typically supported by columns. The inside of the triangle is called the tympanum. Example: 227 King Street South, Page 17	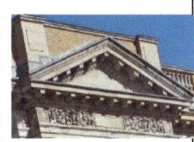

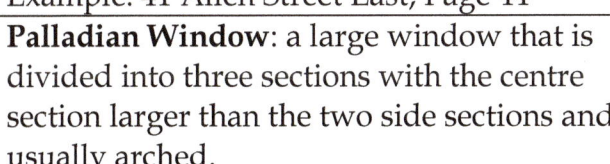

Quoin: masonry blocks at the corner of a wall, often a decorative feature, usually larger or of a different colour than the rest of the wall. Example: 227 King Street South, Page 17	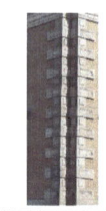
Sidelight: a window, usually with a vertical emphasis, that flanks a door, and is often used to emphasize the importance of a primary entrance. **Transom Window:** the light above the doorway, also called a fanlight. Example: 65 George Street, see Page 29	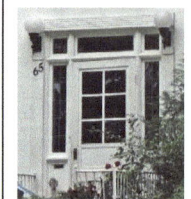
Turret: a small tower that projects from the wall of a building. Example: 203 Mary Street, Page 47	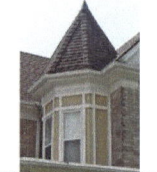
Verge board and Finial: also called bargeboards – hang from the projecting end of a roof and are often elaborately carved and ornamented. **Finial:** ornament added to the top of a gable, pinnacle, canopy or spire – a Gothic element. Example: 172 King Street South, Page 15	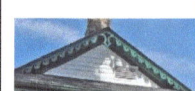

Building Styles

Arts and Crafts: The overlying theme - the house was based on the function of the house. Rooms were oriented to take advantage of the movement of the sun for warmth and light during daylight hours. Side entrances allowed for useable space on the front facade for light or garden use. Arts and Crafts houses have many of these features: wood, stone or stucco siding; low-pitched roof; wide eaves with triangular brackets; exposed roof rafters; porch with thick square or round columns; stone porch supports; exterior chimney made with stone; open floor plans with few hallways; many windows, some with stained or leaded glass; beamed ceilings; dark wood wainscoting and moldings; built-in cabinets, shelves, and seating. Example: 208 King Street South, see Page 21	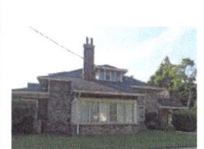
Beaux Arts: Promoters of this style sought to express the classical principles on a grand and imposing scale. Many of the Beaux Arts buildings were banks, post offices, and railway stations. The Ontario Beaux Arts style is eclectic mixing elements of Classical, Renaissance and Baroque. Often the designs have a temple-like façade, pedimented porticos, balustrades, capitals in many styles. Example: 75 Allen Street East, see Page 38	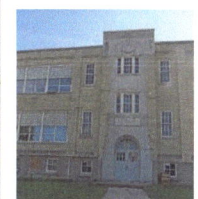

Classical Revival (1820 - 1860) – This style was an analytical, scientific, and dogmatic revival based on intensive studies of Greek and Roman buildings, concerned with the application of Greek plans and proportions to civic buildings. Schools, libraries, government offices, and most other civic buildings were built in the Classical Revival style. The white columned porches of the Classical Revival domestic buildings are identified with the mansions of wealthy land owners in Canada. Example: 160 King Street South, see Page 12	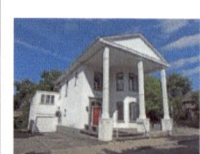
Edwardian, 1900-1930 – This style bridges the ornate and elaborate styles of the Victorian era and the simplified styles of the 20th century. Balanced facades, simple roof lines, dormer windows, large front porches, and smooth brick surfaces are its characteristics. Example: 59 George Street, see Page 31	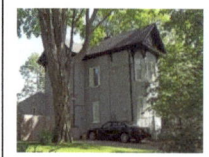
An English country house is a large house or mansion usually unfortified. Example: 31 Union Street East, Page 51	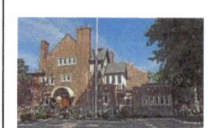

Georgian, before 1860 – This style began with the British King Georges in the 18th century. These buildings have balanced facades around a central door, medium-pitched gable roofs, and small paned windows. Example: 67 Allen Street East, see Page 40	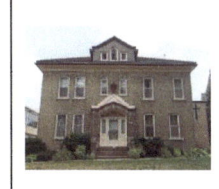
Gothic Revival, 1830-1890 – These decorative buildings have sharply-pitched gables with highly detailed verge boards, pointed-arch window openings, and dichromatic brickwork. It is a common style in Ontario. Example: 28 George Street, see Page 27	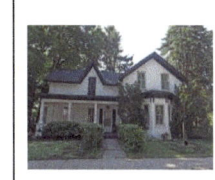
Italianate, 1850-1900 – It has wide-bracketed eaves, belvederes, wrap-around verandahs. Example: 156 King Street South, Page 11	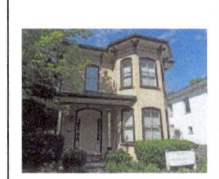
Queen Anne, 1885-1900 – This style is distinguished by an irregular outline featuring a combination of an offset tower, broad gables, projecting two-storey bays, verandahs, multi-sloped roofs, and tall, decorative chimneys. A mixture of brick and wood is common. Windows often have one large single-paned bottom sash and small panes in the upper sash. Example: 189 Mary Street, see Page 45	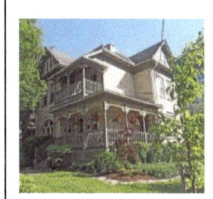

Renaissance Revival (1870 - 1910) - The Renaissance Palazzo was a three or four storey building with a rusticated (very large masonry blocks with deep joints and decorated with rough or bold finishes) ground floor, and regularized understated windows on two upper levels, always finished by an elaborate cornice. The Renaissance saw the development of a graceful and balanced adaptation of the Greek styles. In Ontario, the Renaissance was revived in commercial buildings, banks, offices, and churches in many towns. Most of the Renaissance Revival buildings are designed without columns while those with columns and pilasters are more ornate. Example: 227 King Street South, see Page 17	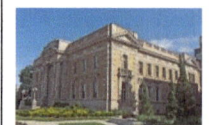
Romanesque Revival, 1880-1910 – This style hearkens back to medieval architecture of the 11th and 12th centuries with a heavy appearance, blocky towers and rounded arches. Example: Mary Street, see Page 48	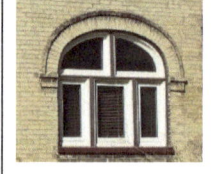

Vernacular/Traditional Mode 1638 - 1950 Influenced but not defined by a particular style, vernacular buildings are made from easily available materials and exhibit local design characteristics. Example: 8 William Street East, see Page 11	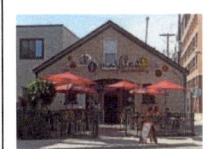
Victorian - In Ontario, a Victorian style building can be seen as any building built between 1840 and 1900 that doesn't fit into any of the other categories. It encompasses a large group of buildings constructed in brick, stone, and timber, using an eclectic mixture of Classical and Gothic motifs. Example: 88 William Street West, see Page 9	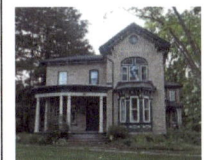

www.ingramcontent.com/pod-product-compliance
Lightning Source LLC
Chambersburg PA
CBHW040843180526
45159CB00001B/295